Francis, a New W

Francis, a New World Pope

Michel Cool

Translated by Regan Kramer

WILLIAM B. EERDMANS PUBLISHING COMPANY

GRAND RAPIDS, MICHIGAN / CAMBRIDGE, U.K.

First published in French as *François, Pape du Nouveau Monde*
© 2013 Éditions Salvator, Paris

English translation © 2013 Wm. B. Eerdmans Publishing Co.
All rights reserved

Published 2013 by
Wm. B. Eerdmans Publishing Co.
2140 Oak Industrial Drive N.E., Grand Rapids, Michigan 49505 /
P.O. Box 163, Cambridge CB3 9PU U.K.
www.eerdmans.com

Printed in the United States of America

19 18 17 16 15 14 13   7 6 5 4 3 2 1

Library of Congress Cataloging-in-Publication Data
ISBN 978-0-8028-7100-8

All quotes from Pope Benedict XVI and Pope Francis, as popes, are in the translation from www.vatican.va/.

Contents

Mercy on the March

Since his historic election on March 13, 2013, Pope Francis has been revealing a new feature of his complex and endearing personality every day. He is letting the world see him as he is, in a kind of echo of the intimate and overwhelming event he experienced inside the Sistine Chapel. For there he let himself be looked upon by Jesus Christ when the cardinals decisively chose to cast their ballots for him. Then, when he accepted the task confided in him — becoming the 266th man at the helm of Saint Peter's bark — he let himself be fetched by the Savior who, from that moment on, would never cease asking him, every single morning of his pontificate, "Francis, do you love me?"

Surprising the waiting throngs with his bashful smile, displayed during his first appearance on the balcony of the Vatican's basilica, was only the first step. Since then he has been ceaselessly establishing the unprecedented style — both plain and contemplative — of the papacy of the first Supreme Pontiff from the New World. And so we saw him lay a bouquet of flowers before an icon of the Virgin Mary, as little children do to honor their Mother in the Sky. We saw him pay his bill like any other client at the hotel he stayed at before the conclave. We saw him burst out laughing inside the Vatican, lightening up the austere and foreboding atmosphere that usually reigns in that ancient and solemn Roman palace. And this tango-loving Argentine who has become the new Vicar of Christ surely has other surprises in store for us. If all of them come to pass, no one will ever again be able to doubt that the Holy Spirit is able to guide his Church through these rough seas by providing it with a captain able to stay the course toward hope.

"God never tires of forgiving us, never! . . . We are the ones who tire of asking forgiveness. . . . He is the loving Father who always forgives, who has that heart of mercy for all of us. . . . Mercy changes everything. . . . A bit of mercy makes the world less cold and more just!" That was the message — like an ode to divine mercy — delivered to the thousands of pilgrims who had come to Saint Peter's Square to listen to and applaud Pope Francis's first Angelus address. Is this pope the harbinger of the Revolution of Mercy that the desperadoes of our era of upheaval have been longing for?

With a bit of patience, we will soon know if this man, with his apparent simplicity, this simply human man, will indeed ring in the Revolution of Mercy that was so dear to the Saint of Assisi, whose name he has adopted. For that Francis was the apostle and the witness, the servant as demanding and luminous as a diamond to the poor, the meek, and the humble.

"Pray for me," the new pope tells all he meets. It was already his leitmotiv as archbishop of Buenos Aires. What if we took his petition literally? If, like him, and after so many saints before him, we decided to put our faith in faith? If we too finally staked our all on the strength of prayer to bring about the advent of this Revolution of Mercy that we all need, and to which this pope who has come halfway around the world to serve seems to want to open the path?

On his journey toward mercy, Pope Francis will need the cooperation of all men and women of good will. So this is the incredible adventure on which we have been invited to join Francis, the New World pope, whose portrait and history this book presents.

CHAPTER I

Francis and the Seagull

Wednesday, March 13, 2013: It's raining on Rome. Cameramen from TV stations around the world have trained their lenses on the Sistine Chapel's silent chimney. They are being entertained by a seagull's unexpected choreography. The incongruous bird is strolling across the roof of the sacred edifice, indifferent to the surrounding excitement. No one will ever know if the bird is called Jonathan, like the hero of the book from the 1970s. But this seafaring, well-traveled bird will go down in history. Because whether it's just a coincidence, or more likely, a sign from God, didn't its appearance foretell the election of a pope who sailed the seas to come here, to the banks of the Tiber River, to pilot the bark of the Church?

A throng of some 100,000 people is standing patiently on the cobblestones of Saint Peter's Square. They stare at the sky, hoping for a wisp of white smoke. Their patience will not be in vain. Just before 7 P.M., thick curls of white smoke rise up from the copper chimney. A few long minutes later, the cardinal-deacon, Frenchman Jean-Louis Tauran, appears on the central balcony of Saint Peter's Basilica to announce the joyful news: *"Habemus papam!"* Still speaking Latin, he reveals the identity of the chosen one. After a moment of hesitation, as though the crowd is stunned by what it has just heard, a huge shout rises up. The clamor soon becomes an acclamation of joy, a surge of jubilation. The seagull has disappeared from television screens. It has flown away, we know not where, taking the mystery of its presence on this historic evening with it.

Francis! The name of the man in white who is stepping onto Saint Peter's benediction loggia is Francis, like the saint from Assisi. And there is yet another surprise on top of that first one: he has forgone the scarlet *mozzetta* the pontiff traditionally wears on his shoulders. In a slow, deep voice, he starts by wishing everyone "Good evening," raising his hand to greet the crowd who has come to welcome him. "Dear brothers, dear sisters," he begins, in Italian, warmly addressing the enthusiastic pilgrims waving signs and banners to glorify the Holy Father.

His face is filled with emotion, but at peace, his arms at his side, his attitude during his first appearance as pope displays a key feature of his personality: his no-frills side. "It seems," he goes on with a cheerful grin, "that my brother Cardinals have gone to the ends of the earth to get [me] . . . but here we are. . . . I thank you for your welcome." Then he invites everyone to join him in prayer, as he offers an Our Father and a Hail Mary for his predecessor, Benedict XVI, who is surely watching the scene on TV in Castel Gandolfo, to which he retired when he renounced the papacy on February 28, 2013.

Those first few words and gestures suffice to create a direct, warm contact between the new bishop of Rome and the people of his city. The bond is already palpable on Saint Peter's Square: despite the falling darkness, the people's faces are radiant, and their eyes sparkle like a constellation of stars. The new Vicar of Christ compares this budding relationship with the people of Rome to a journey of brotherhood, of love, and of evangelization. Then comes another exceptionally moving moment: the 265th successor to Saint Peter invites the faithful to ask for the Lord's blessing for him. He bows down to the multitude, which prays in silence for twenty seconds or so. This is unheard of! Never in their long history have Bernini's columns borne witness to such a profound silence, so filled with fervor and hope to greet the arrival of a Supreme Pontiff.

The Cardinals' Historic Choice

It's a huge surprise. This election is absolutely historic! Against all odds, and for the first time since the eighth century, a pontiff from a continent other than Europe has been elected. By placing the Argentinean archbishop of Buenos Aires, Jorge Mario Bergoglio, on Saint Peter's throne, the 115 cardinals elected "the first pope from the Americas," as President Barack Obama, one of the first to offer his best wishes to the new pontiff, put it. Another first, this pope could be described as "black" in a way. He belongs to the Society of Jesus, whose superior, called Father General, is also known as "the black pope" because of the black cassock he wears, as opposed to the bishop of Rome's white tunic. So Pope Francis is also the first Jesuit pope of the Catholic Church since Saint Ignatius of Loyola founded that religious order in the sixteenth century. That's a lot of innovation for a single seventy-six-year-old man! Yet he wasn't even considered *papabile* (a possible pope) going into this conclave.

First non-European pope in thirteen centuries; first New World pope since Christopher Columbus discovered it in the fifteenth century; and finally, first-ever Jesuit pope of the Roman Catholic Church. Yet he was elected quickly, on only the fifth round of voting, on just the second day of the bishops' seclusion in the Sistine Chapel. He was elected even more quickly than Paul VI, who was the frontrunner of the conclave in 1963, and his election was almost as easy as Benedict XVI's, who had been chosen on the fourth round in 2005. For Father Federico Lombardi, a Jesuit himself, and director of the Holy See Press Office, the cardinal electors — with the help and guidance of the Holy Spirit — showed truly bold initiative on March 13, 2013: "I was dumbfounded," he said. "They were brave enough to look across the ocean to broaden the Church's perspectives."

It's a bold choice, but it also reflects the reality of demographic changes in the Catholic world; their choice reflects the changing center of gravity in global Catholicism over the past few decades. The largest number of the faithful do in fact live in the Southern Hemisphere now, and that is where the faith still draws huge crowds into churches and pilgrimage centers. The election of a South American pope does indeed symbolize the end of the Old World's 2,000-year hold on the See of Peter; but more than that, it is an act of recognition — recognition that, although the Church is still universal, and alive on every continent, its heart and soul are now to be found in the emerging countries of the South.

The world's leaders grasped that instantly. Recognizing the historic dimension of the event, they reacted quickly to Pope Francis's surprising election. Barack Obama, head of the world's premier superpower, was one of the first to send his "warm wishes" to the new pontiff, praising him as a "champion of the poor and the most vulnerable among us." UN Secretary-General Ban Ki-moon expressed his hope that, like his predecessor, Benedict XVI, the new pope would continue to promote interfaith dialogue. "We also share the conviction that we can only resolve the interconnected challenges of today's world through dialogue."

Several Latin American heads of state spoke of their people's pride and joy that one of their own had been elected to the papacy. Even Cristina Kirchner, the president of Argentina, set aside her political differences with the former archbishop of Buenos Aires — who had been seen as her principal adversary — to salute the election of a fellow countryman. With an admirable sense of fair play, she wished him well with his "great responsibility toward advancing justice, equality, fraternity and peace of mankind."

In what was perhaps an attempt to change the unfortunate impression he had made by joking about Benedict XVI's retirement, François Hollande was one of the first European leaders to present the new Supreme Pontiff with his "most sincere wishes for the important mission that has just been confided in him." The French president then added: "France, true to its history and to the universal principles of liberty, equality and fraternity that found its action throughout the world, will continue the trustful dialogue it has always maintained with the Holy See, in the service of peace, justice, solidarity and human dignity."

Among the many diplomatic telegrams sent to Pope Francis, it is worth mentioning the one from the Israeli president Shimon Peres, inviting Francis to Israel on an official visit, as well as the press release from the European Union, cosigned by the president of the European Council, Herman Van Rompuy, and the president of the European Commission, José Manuel Barroso, wishing him a "long and blessed" pontificate so that he could "defend and promote the fundamental human values of peace, solidarity and human dignity."

Clearly, governments were not blind to the wave of hope and enthusiasm sparked by Francis's election. An unexpected one, it must be said, foreseen neither by the specialized press nor even by Latin American public opinion. The populace there had lost faith in the chances of the "poor people's archbishop," as he was known in the underprivileged neigh-borhoods of Buenos Aires. So how did Cardinal Bergoglio unexpectedly leave the Sistine Chapel as the Vicar of Christ?

How Bergoglio's Name Rose to the Top

Tongues had wagged to the press after the 2005 conclave, sharing information about what had gone on behind those locked doors. They said that Jorge Mario Bergoglio had at-tracted enough votes to be considered Cardinal Joseph Ratz-inger's strongest competitor. According to those rumors, the Argentinean prelate enjoyed the support of the liberal wing of the College of Cardinals. At that time, their leader was the late archbishop of Milan and eminent Jesuit scholar Carlo Maria Martini, who even then was fighting the rare form of incurable Parkinson's disease that would cut him down in 2012.

But Bergoglio dampened his supporters' ardor by claim-ing to be in poor health. Indeed, ever since the Argentine had lost a lung to the tuberculosis he had contracted in his youth, he had needed to watch himself. He also said he didn't want to prevent the election of Ratzinger, whose lofty intel-lect he admired, and who could lay claim to the role of John Paul II's natural successor. Still, a number of cardinals at that conclave were impressed with their Argentinean counter-part's eminent spiritual and pastoral qualities. Intransigent when it came to Catholic moral doctrine, Bergoglio was equally firm about the Church's social doctrine. His greatest asset is to incarnate a synthesis between, on the one hand, the tenets of doctrinal conservatism opposed to widespread liberalization of social mores, and on the other, the vision of a social Catholicism that would stand up to the excesses of an unbridled global economy under the sway of the financial powers that be.

That same duality seems to have determined the outcome eight years later. And yet the Argentinean cardinal has aged: he is just two years younger than Benedict XVI was when he was elected, in April 2005. And his health is no less affected now by his missing lung than it was then. One might easily assume that the reasons Pope Benedict gave for relinquishing his position would lead the cardinals to choose a younger, more vigorous successor. According to the French cardinals, the issue of their next leader's age was indeed debated at the conclave, before the first vote and between votes, yet clearly, in the end, it didn't prevent the election of the outsider Bergoglio.

So just what were the decisive criteria in choosing him? We can suggest four that were in his favor:

1. His personal aura, which had not weakened since the previous conclave.
2. Both his international stature and his reputation as a man who knows how to network, which were shown or reinforced by several elements: his Italian descent — which would comfort the Italian and European car-

dinals who might mourn the historic loss of the papacy if a non-European were elected; his membership in a religious order with outposts around the world; and his close ties to the Communion and Liberation movement, which is very influential in Italy.

3. His pastoral sense and his intelligence, as well as his spiritual depth and personal modesty, also helped bring consensus to their eminences, as the cardinals are sometimes referred to. He was also appreciated by the Roman Curia, which he was a part of, having been a member of several Roman congregations and both a pontifical commission and a pontifical council.

4. His diocese's focus on evangelizing in the streets, the slums, and other places considered distant from the church, and on getting priests and the laity to work together, could well galvanize priests searching for the inspiration and means to reenergize their communities.

It also helped him that, during the general congregations preceding the conclave, the cardinals had clearly stated their desire to turn the page on the Roman Curia's dysfunctions and the scandals that had recently tarnished the Church's image and credibility. Taken all together, it began to look like a red carpet had been laid at Cardinal Bergoglio's feet. Because, in addition to his renowned integrity, his natural authority — unblemished by the least trace of authoritarianism or scorn — was recognized and respected by all.

In the less troubled context of Benedict XVI's succession, less tragic or traumatic than the prevailing mood during John Paul II's, Bergoglio's name gradually drew the attention of the cardinal electors. They seem not to have been disposed to elect either an Italian or any candidate who was supported, even discreetly, by the "bosses" of the Curia who were worried about their own future. And so — without of course minimizing the inspiration of the prayers chanted during the impressive, hours-long liturgy experienced by participants in a conclave — after five rounds of balloting, an Argentinean Jesuit wound up in the Room of Tears donning the white cassock of the successors to the Prince of Apostles.

Who Is Jorge Mario Bergoglio?

The new pope was born on December 17, 1936, in downtown Buenos Aires. His family, of modest means, had Italian roots, like many people in the Argentinean capital. His father, Mario, from Torino, in the Piedmont region, was an accountant for a railroad company. His mother, Regina Sivori, was from Genoa, on the Ligurian coast. A full-time housewife, she raised five children.

Jorge Mario started out at the local public school. His original goal had been to become a chemist. But at the age of seventeen, he had a powerful spiritual experience that affected him deeply, changing the path of his life. He was taking confession in his parish church when the priest's words touched him to his core and steered him toward a religious vocation. Ever since he was ordained as a priest, Jorge Mario Bergoglio has commemorated the memory of this sudden vocation by celebrating an Easter Mass in the church where it was revealed to him.

The young man soon decided to change his lifestyle: no more dancing the tango with his friends in the bars of Buenos Aires, and no more dating his girlfriend, either. In 1958, at the age of twenty-two, he quit his job analyzing food in a laboratory and entered the novitiate of the Society of Jesus. He was ordained to the priesthood eleven years later, after a long literary, philosophical, and theological formation that took him to Chile and to Germany, where he wrote his doctoral thesis in that country's language. Upon his return to Argentina, he was assigned to minister to a provincial parish some 400 miles north of the capital. In April 1973 he pronounced his final, perpetual Jesuit vows. In July of the same year, he was named provincial superior, in other words, the highest-ranking Jesuit in Argentina, a position he held for six years under very difficult circumstances.

The implacable military dictatorship that ruled the country from 1976 to 1983 brought violence and suffering to the whole of Argentinean society. The fact that part of the Catholic hierarchy was in collusion with the junta fanned divisions and sowed discord within the Church. The Society of Jesus was not spared the bitter debates between partisans of an effective resistance and a liberation theology that advocated violent action, and others, including Bergoglio, who rejected excessive politicization of their faith, defending the spirituality of their order above all. Did his superiors take umbrage over his position during the "Dirty War," as the Argentines refer to this sinister period? Or did they blame him for his lack of solidarity during the standoff in Rome between Father Pedro Arrupe, the Jesuit superior general and an emblematic figure of the "preferential option for the poor," and Pope John Paul II? For the Polish pope disapproved of what he saw as an unholy alliance between some Jesuits and the Marxist theoreticians of liberation theology. According to those inside, Bergoglio, whose career had followed a meteoric path until then, suddenly found himself in something of a wilderness starting in the early 1980s. The dry spell lasted a dozen years. Rector of first a provincial faculty, then a seminary; professor; parish priest; convent chaplain — the Jesuit whose ideas went against the prevailing winds did as he was told, honoring his vows of obedience, and persevering, as was his wont.

In 1992 he was admitted back into the fold. At the age of fifty-six, this "hard-line Wojtilian," as one of his biographers put it, was appointed titular bishop of Auca and auxiliary bishop of Buenos Aires by John Paul II. After that, he rose through the ranks of the Catholic hierarchy in the Argentinean capital, succeeding Cardinal Antonio as archbishop of Buenos Aires in 1998. A few days before Antonio died, the elderly cardinal welcomed the news of Bergoglio's appointment, painting the portrait of a "discreet but very efficient man, loyal to the Church and very close both to the priests and to the Catholic faithful."

One of the first decisions made by the new archbishop was to forgo the luxurious residence that came with his position and to live in a small apartment near the cathedral. Profits from the sale of the episcopal palace were distributed to charitable organizations. By the same token, he declined to use a chauffeur-driven car, instead taking the bus or subway like everybody else. "My parishioners are poor and I am one of them," he said to explain his lifestyle. In 2001, this archbishop with the austere — one might even say ascetic — lifestyle was created a cardinal by John Paul.

Without Christ's Mercy

As pope, Jorge Mario Bergoglio chose to keep the bishop's pectoral cross engraved with the image of the Good Shepherd around his neck. It even seems likely that Pope Francis will keep his episcopal motto, *Miserando atque eligendo,* which means "by making mercy and by choosing." But it could also be translated as "making mercy and choosing to practice it." The phrase is taken from a homily of Saint Bede, a Doctor of the Church (intellectual and spiritual master), also known as the Venerable Bede, who lived in England in the eighth century, a period thought of as the High Middle Ages. In Bede's text, he comments on the conversion of a "publican" (the name for tax collectors in Roman times; universally despised, they were also thought of as corrupt) who turns out to be the future apostle and evangelist Saint Matthew. "So

Jesus looked at the publican, and because he looked at him as an object of mercy (i.e., with his heart filled with pity and compassion) and of predilection, Jesus said to the publican, 'Follow me!' "

The choice of this particular excerpt to inspire his episcopal motto clearly indicates Pope Francis's priorities: as the son of Italian emigrants — as well as out of fidelity to the gospel — he is instinctively close to those who are rejected and scorned, the outcast victims of discrimination. Like Francis of Assisi, who kissed a leper, this Vicar of Christ exhorts bishops, priests, and the laity to step out of their sacristies and chapels and to go bear authentic witness for Christ among those who are wounded and crushed by poverty and who despair of ever recovering their human dignity.

For the priests in Buenos Aires whom he met during his pastoral visits, Archbishop Bergoglio had three main recommendations, which he repeated endlessly, hammering home his message without shouting or even raising his voice, but simply by exercising the natural authority of those who practice what they preach. His three recommendations: practice mercy, have apostolic courage, and make yourself available to all. Although he has a generally shy and retiring manner, as archbishop he was occasionally known to change his tone to criticize a priest or a pastoral leader's inappropriate, unreasonable, or unfair behavior. For instance, one day he lost his temper over the "neoclericalism" of certain priests in his diocese who, in his opinion, were diverting the sacraments from their true purpose by refusing to baptize the children of single mothers. Denying baptism to children born outside of wedlock is, in his words, a kind of "Pharisaic Gnosticism" that drives people away from salvation and discourages them from taking the promises of happiness and liberation announced in the Gospel seriously. "I say this with sadness, and if it sounds like a complaint or an offensive comment please forgive me: in our ecclesiastical region there are presbyteries that will not baptize children whose mothers are not married because the infants were conceived outside of holy wedlock," he declared in September 2012. "They are the hypocrites of our times. They clericalize the Church. They drive God's people away from salvation. Think of that poor girl who beat the temptation instilled by some in her to abort, who had the courage to bring her child into the world, then found herself on a pilgrimage, going from parish to parish, trying to find someone who would baptize her child."

As a Jesuit accustomed to spiritual exercises, he starts each day with an hour of silent prayer. In 2001, as an archbishop able to arrange his schedule so he could hear his parishioners' confession, to give them the holy sacraments and allow them to attend saints' day celebrations, he gave us a glimpse of what those moments of personal contemplation brought him. "Only someone who has encountered mercy, who has been caressed by the tenderness of mercy, is happy and comfortable with the Lord," he confided.

Prayer is the secret pacifying weapon of this pastor who is always on the go, ready to come to the fore and bear witness to the joy and faith that animate him at all times. Even in the most bitter battles he has fought — against Argentinean president Cristina Kirchner's same-sex marriage legislation, for example — he enjoined the faithful not to tire of prayer, but to have faith in its transformative force and power to convert. In 2010 he wrote a letter along those lines to the contemplative communities in his diocese:

> I recall the words of Saint Thérèse of the Child Jesus as she speaks of the infirmity of her childhood. She said that the devil's jealousy sought revenge on her family after her older sister joined the Carmel. Here too, is jealousy of the Devil, through which sin came into the world: jealousy that deceitfully tries to destroy God's image, that is man and woman who receive the commandment to be fruitful and to multiply, and to govern the earth. . . . And that is why I am calling upon you and asking you for prayers and sacrifice, Saint Teresa's two invincible weapons. Cry out to the Lord that he may send his spirit to the Senators who have said they will vote. That they not do it under the sway of error or contingent circumstances, but according to what natural law and God's law show them. Pray for them and their families. That God may visit them, strengthen them and comfort them. Pray that the Senators do great good for our Nation.

As archbishop of Buenos Aires, he routinely asked people to pray for him. The night of his election, Pope Francis didn't change his habits: the people of Rome were invited to pray for their new bishop. And so they found out that, for this kneeling pontiff, "Without Christ's Mercy" — to quote the title of the Franco-Argentinean author Hector Bianciotti's famous novel — there is no credible brotherhood, evangelization, or bearing Christian witness.

A Good Listener, in Touch with His Flock

"It is in *giving* that we *receive*," Saint Francis of Assisi — to whom the new pope has dedicated his pontificate — said to his earliest companions. But even before he became pope, in Buenos Aires, Cardinal Bergoglio was known for giving a great deal of his time to the priests of his diocese, whom he welcomed and visited, and above all, whom he listened to. Taking Dom Hélder Câmara (1909-99), an intrepid defender of human rights, as his role model, he shunned the archbishop's residence offered to him, and chose instead to live in a modest apartment without a maid or a cook. "He listens twice as much as he speaks and notices a lot more than what he hears," someone close to him explained to *La Croix,* a French Catholic newspaper, in 2005. To facilitate communication with the clergy, he installed a direct phone line so they could reach him more easily. He also corresponded online, and often surprised people with the speed of his replies. "When you left a message, he would get back to you right away," a priest remembers.

Well organized and methodical, the cardinal primate of

Argentina made it a point of honor to start his day by chatting with priests from his diocese. To find the time to do that, he would rise before dawn, at 4:30 A.M. After an hour devoted to prayer and a half hour to get some reading done, he received priests every day from 6 to 8. The only requirement to visit him was to be an early riser! He would also frequently have lunch with one of them, and every weekend he would go to a different church in his diocese to celebrate mass and to meet the parish's vital forces. In solidarity with a priest in the slums who had received death threats from drug dealers, he stayed at that priest's home. He demanded the same apostolic courage from himself as he did from his collaborators.

A good listener who doesn't cut himself off from people, Jorge Mario Bergoglio isn't talkative, except when he is dispensing homilies denouncing political corruption or the crisis of values in Argentinean society. Otherwise, he is humble enough to keep his mouth shut, and to prefer to sit toward the back of an assembly, rather than up in the front row. One of the first things he did when elevated to the cardinalate in June 2001 was to ask the Argentinean embassy to the Holy See not to organize the fancy receptions that were customary on that sort of occasion. By the same token, he suggested that his friends and relatives who wanted to come to Rome to celebrate the event should donate the cost of the journey to charity instead.

Humility is the cardinal virtue of a Christian life, and it can be excellent advice for a society or even a country as well. In a homily delivered on May 25, 2011, an important

Argentinean patriotic holiday, the cardinal did in fact declare that "humility reveals the potential trapped inside human smallness. By being aware of both our own gifts and our own limitations, we free ourselves of the blindness of pride. And just as Jesus praised our Father for the revelation made to the meek, we should also praise our Father for making the May sun rise on those who trust in the gift of freedom, the freedom that grows inside the hearts of a people that wagers on greatness without losing sight of its own smallness." The bishop of Troyes, a city in eastern France, who had a chance to spend an hour with Bergoglio during a trip to Buenos Aires as president of the France–Latin America Episcopal Committee (CEFAL), said he was struck by the "quiet strength of humility" that emanates from this man who is well versed in the reality of his own history, but also of his own potential and limits. "What he wants, it seems to me," the Frenchman added, "is a credible Church that, like him, isn't afraid to recognize its own limits, yet without giving in, or giving up on moving forward and changing."

This man who has had such a singular life journey still suffers poor health. He has had just one lung since he was operated on at age twenty. This physical handicap brings him a sense of closeness to the sick, the elderly, and the fragile, whom he frequently visits in hospitals. He was seen at the bedside of victims of the terrible nightclub fire in Buenos Aires in late 2004.

He also regularly visits overlooked places in the capital: slums and prisons. He has deliberately doubled the number of priests in those neighborhoods that are so often abandoned to the drug dealers. Last year, during Holy Week, he washed the feet of a dozen young drug addicts in a working-class neighborhood called Bajo Flores. He has shown deep compassion for people with AIDS: in 2001, he visited a hospice care center and washed the feet of patients there. "He really knew what was going on in the streets of our neighborhoods," his priests said admiringly — if sadly, as they are now feeling somewhat orphaned.

Both Kind and Shrewd

Shortly after Benedict XVI's resignation, the archbishop of Paris, Cardinal André Vingt-Trois, suggested that the pope who emerged from the upcoming conclave would need a double profile: someone who was good and holy, but who also had a sharp political sense and was quite shrewd. Has that prediction come true? Pope Francis's first steps in public have revealed a man with a real and wonderful authenticity about him, but one who also knows how to make a statement — in words and deeds — that has been cleverly thought through and is rich with meaning.

Intellectually speaking, Cardinal Bergoglio was a man to be reckoned with. Like any good Jesuit, he was a cultivated man, whose outlook had been enriched by his extensive travels, his reading, and his taste for movies and opera. His favorite writers are Jorge Luis Borges, Leopoldo Marechal, and

Dostoevsky. When speaking before his brother cardinals, he enjoyed quoting Léon Bloy and a German author, thus displaying the breadth of his reading. As a polyglot, he can read a wide range of books without need for translation. He has himself written a dozen books of reflections and meditations.

Those closest to him say his favorite film is *Babette's Feast*. This Danish film, based on a short story by Karen Blixen and released worldwide in 1987, is generally understood as a celebration of the pleasure of the senses through a meal worthy of the finest French chefs. But it can also be interpreted as a parable about loyalty, sharing, generosity, and selflessness — values that matter to the new pontiff.

Even his obsession with soccer, which is almost a given in a *futbol*-crazed country like Argentina, helps strengthen his ties with young people from the working class. "I haven't missed a single San Lorenzo league game since 1946," the enthusiastic fan confessed in 2010. "The team's colors, blue and red, represent the Virgin's red dress and blue robe," he said. "We took the colors of the Virgin and no others."

Having presided over the Conference of Argentinean Bishops and having participated in sessions of the Latin American Episcopal Council (CELAM), Bergoglio has acquired experience as a man of "good governance." "He displays a strong temperament and a sharp political sense," according to his biographer, the journalist Sergio Rubin. These qualities could help him in maneuvers with the Curia; although he eventually became a part of that body, he did not spend much time there or rise through the ranks. "But his temperament is such that he won't confront them, and they know that," an Argentinean observer says. A different Argentinean observer thinks that, on the contrary, this new pope will bring about change.

"He's a very forthright person," points out his friend, the Argentinean rabbi Abraham Skorka, with whom he cowrote a book. "We share the conviction that it is by respecting humanity that you become close to God," adds this leader of a large Jewish congregation in Buenos Aires. That community is now waiting for the new pope to go beyond speechifying and to take concrete steps toward a true rapprochement with the Church's "older brothers."

Open-minded about social issues, he frequently assails social exclusion and corruption among the elites. But as a cardinal, he never expressed any differences with Benedict XVI, whose doctrinal strictness in private morals and ecclesiastical discipline he shares. In Argentina, he vocally defended the Church's traditional stance on married priests and abortion. And he spearheaded the opposition to same-sex marriage — in vain. Jorge Mario Bergoglio also spoke out against allowing transsexuals to change their gender on their IDs. Since those battles, he has been in open conflict with the Argentinean president, Cristina Kirchner. "If the Church wants to be progressive," he proclaimed in Quebec, in 2008, "it has to acknowledge, and not deny, its historical heritage, and then move forward. If we say that in order to be progressive, the Church has to keep up with every passing ideology, then it will lose its identity and turn into an NGO."

The one indisputable skeleton in his closet: the cardinal's controversial attitude during Argentina's "Dirty War." The Argentinean church, which Bergoglio led before becoming the new pope, is one of the most highly criticized ones in South America, for its passivity toward — if not out-and-out complicity with — the last military dictatorship (1976-83). National Catholicism was the dominant ideology of the armed forces, and for this they received the Church hierarchy's blessing. Unlike the churches in Brazil and Chile, which played key roles in defending victims of repression and in the struggle for freedom, the Argentinean Catholic hierarchy showed a culpable indifference to the horrors committed.

The priests and nuns who outspokenly declared their solidarity with the Madres de la Plaza de Mayo, the spokeswomen for the families of the some 30,000 "disappeared," were on their own. They were not supported by their hierarchy, and some of them paid for their opposition to the dictatorship with their lives. In 2000, Christianity's jubilee year, Bergoglio asked his Church to recognize its role during the dictatorship and called for it to do penance in order to clean the stain from its name. Nevertheless, in 2005, a virulent diatribe accusing him of having collaborated with the junta and turned in priests was published in Argentina just a few days before the start of the conclave that elected Benedict XVI — after very nearly choosing Bergoglio. Questioned by the police, the cardinal vigorously denied those accusations, providing documents to prove his statements. Even the artist and human-rights activist Adolfo Perez Esquivel, the 1980 Nobel Peace Prize winner and a man who is above suspicion of collusion with the dictatorship, has cleared Bergoglio's name of any collaboration with the military junta. On March 13, 2013, Perez Esquivel told the BBC, "I know personally that a number of bishops did ask the junta to release prisoners and priests, and their requests were not granted." He himself spent fourteen months in prison, where he was tortured, without ever being tried, and was then freed, spending another fourteen months under close surveillance. While in jail, he received the John XXIII Peace Memorial, awarded by Pax Christi International.

What pastoral legacy will the former archbishop of Buenos Aires leave behind? First and foremost, he is remembered as someone who thought strategically, and was concerned with adapting the local Church's evangelization methods to the new realities of a megalopolis of more than 3 million inhabitants like Buenos Aires. In an interview granted in 2012 to an Italian Vatican specialist, Cardinal Bergoglio laid out the goals he had assigned to his pastoral agents, be they clergy or laity:

> We try to get in touch with families who are not involved in their parish. Instead of being a Church that simply welcomes all those who seek it out, we try to be a Church that goes beyond its walls and reaches out towards men and women who don't share in parish life, who might not

know much about it or who are indifferent to it. We organize evangelization missions in public places where people
congregate. We usually pray, celebrate Mass and offer baptism after administering a quick preparation. In addition,
we also try to open up to those who are far from us, using
digital communication tools like the web, instant messag-
ing, etc.

Cardinal Bergoglio also leaves behind a missionary project focused on communication and evangelization, which is
of course unfinished. It will continue to pursue four goals:

1. Found open, fraternal communities.
2. Encourage the active participation of trained laity.
3. Offer the gospel to every inhabitant of the city.
4. Reinforce solidarity with the poor and the sick.

In 2009, as part of the bicentennial celebration of Argentinean independence, Bergoglio launched a huge fund-
raising campaign. The goal was to open 200 new charities
by 2016. In fact, the future Pope Francis was applying the
directives set in 2007 by the Latin American bishops' conference — which was held at Our Lady of Aparecida, the
shrine to the patron saint of Brazil — at home. In the conference's concluding document, the bishops declared that "the
Church is called to make all its members disciples and missionaries of Christ, Way, Truth and Life, so our peoples may
have life in Him."

"... Sibi Nomen Imposuit Francisum ..."

"He takes to himself the name of Francis": Cardinal Tauran's announcement of the new pope's name was one of the other major surprises on that historic evening of March 13, 2013. It was the first time in Church history that a Supreme Pontiff had chosen that name. Many commentators wondered out loud who the new pope wanted to honor in this way. Was it Francis of Assisi, the most venerated saint in the church and the most popular one in the world? The thirteenth-century founder of the mendicant order of the Franciscans is beloved for his simple lifestyle and his goodness to the poor and downtrodden of his time, like lepers. Or could it be Saint Francis Xavier, a sixteenth-century Spanish Jesuit priest whose extraordinary missionary zeal took him all the way to China? Another Jesuit from the same period was also mentioned as a possible namesake: Francis Borgia, who contributed greatly to the Society's expansion around the world. Lastly, the name of Saint Francis of Sales, a seventeenth-century spiritual master who never separated the Church's evangelizing mission from its charitable duties, was considered.

Father Federico Lombardi put an end to the speculation by declaring that the new pope had chosen his name in honor of Saint Francis of Assisi. "Francis" was also the Supreme Pontiff's own father's third given name: Jorge Mario Francisco.

In the meantime, the cheering Argentines had already nicknamed "their pope" Pancho, which is the diminutive for

Francisco in Spanish. A twenty-six-year-old Mexican seminarian who was in attendance at Saint Peter's Square was thrilled with the new Vicar of Christ's name. "Saint Francis gave so much, especially the gift of poverty! In this world, where we have so many things that we don't need, I see the new pope's choice of name as a sign that we need to get back to Christ, our one true wealth." "His name choice of Francis signifies that his papacy will have a great devotion to justice, peace and to the poor," Eric LeCompte — the executive director of Jubilee USA, a religious group that works for financial reform to help the poor — declared in a statement released immediately after the election of Pope Francis. "Here's a guy who has taken the life of St. Francis seriously. He gave up his mansion and driver and lives in an apartment in Buenos Aires."

On March 19, 2013, the day of the inauguration of his pontificate, Pope Francis spoke of every human being's responsibility to protect "each of God's creatures and the environment in which we live . . . as Saint Francis of Assisi showed us." It was a brave choice, because Francis is a demanding name to have, a magnificent one to honor, and one that it is necessary to incarnate in these times of crisis, incertitude, and despair. But perhaps Pope Francis, the new "Servant of the Servants of God," has already had time to meditate on the advice that his namesake, the *Poverello,* gave priests whom he encountered on his path: "Is it not in fact true, that the servants of God are really like jugglers, intended to revive the hearts of men and lead them into spiritual joy?"

CHAPTER II

Ten Pressing Matters

What are the ten most pressing matters requiring Pope Francis's attention? They include both unfinished issues left to him by his predecessor and ones relating to urgent current events. Despite what had been claimed at times, Pope Benedict XVI did not turn out to be a "transition pope." Throughout his pontificate, which was shaken by controversy (Regensburg, Monsignor Williamson) and scandal (Vatileaks), he didn't hesitate to seek the truth on such painful issues for the Church as the Legionaries of Christ and pedophile priests. Now it is up to the new pope to go further and to bring an unprecedented new evangelical momentum to the coming years.

Modernizing the Curia

This is the most urgent issue facing the new leader of the Catholic Church. The cardinal electors have mandated him to strengthen and intensify the reforms that were launched somewhat timidly by Pope Benedict. The Vatileaks scandal deeply affected Benedict and the cardinals. "Never again," swore a respected cardinal just before the start of the conclave. Pope Francis will need to be tremendously firm, tactful, and steadfast in order to refurbish the reputation and efficiency of the Roman Curia, which has been tarnished by these recent scandals. Not since Paul VI (1963-78) has a pope attempted to make any significant changes in how the Roman government of the Catholic Church is run. So old demons are rearing their heads once more: suffocating centralism, lack of communication between different offices and services, careerism, corruption of all sorts, and more.

Of course, the Curia has more honest and devoted collaborators than it has unsavory individuals. But the entrenched Roman administration suffers from structural dysfunctions that mean it's no longer in tune with the contemporary world that local churches are part of. Granted, the Church's perspective is eternity, but as the disastrous Williamson affair made clear, it would do well to improve both its internal information networks and its *urbi et orbi* communication.

What's more, considering that this administration, which represents more than a billion believers around the world, employs a staff of just 5,000, whereas a city like Paris, with 2 million inhabitants, recruits 50,000, those 5,000 clearly need to be highly capable people. But the drop in vocations among European dioceses means they no longer proudly send their best elements to the Vatican as they once did; now the dioceses hold on to their best people to make up for local staff shortages. Clearly, the new pope will need to be both clever and commanding in order to lead the Church to improve its administration, while retaining its essence as a community of believers serving the cause of evangelization — yet without letting it turn into "just another NGO." And indeed, he was just that when he marked his first month as pontiff by naming nine high-ranking prelates to a permanent advisory group to help him run the Church and pave the way for the long-awaited reform of the Vatican bureaucracy. The panel includes only one current Vatican official; the rest are cardinals and a monsignor who hail from six different continents — a bold step toward making the Vatican a truer reflection of the Church's universal nature.

Rekindling Evangelization

Pope Francis has inherited three undertakings begun by his predecessor that he will have to see through to completion. All three are connected to the idea of reviving the proclamation of the gospel, which was the main pastoral priority of the former archbishop of Buenos Aires.

The first one concerns the post-synodal apostolic exhortation that needs to be published following the General Assembly of the Synod of Bishops in Rome in October 2012. The theme of the synod was "The New Evangelization for the Transmission of the Christian Faith." Due to his resignation, Benedict XVI was unable to complete the exhortation.

So it will be up to Francis to take advantage of this solemn text to show the world how he intends to revive the proclamation of Christian faith in the four corners of the globe.

The next important assignment will be the concluding celebration of the Year of Faith, in November 2013. This major initiative had been launched by Benedict in October 2012, in an atmosphere of commemoration of the fiftieth anniversary of the opening of the Second Vatican Council (1962-65). It will be interesting to see how Francis, the first pope of the post-Council generation, will take over that particular role from his predecessor, who had been a key player in that council. Before leaving Rome, Benedict made a point of confiding his memories of that event to the clergymen of the Roman diocese. "And it is our task, especially in this Year of Faith, to work so that the true Council, with its power of the Holy Spirit, be accomplished, and the Church be truly renewed," he said to conclude an entirely improvised speech.

And finally, it may fall to Francis to proceed with the beatification of Paul VI that was initiated by his predecessor at a ceremony during the Year of Faith marking the fiftieth anniversary of the accession of Jean-Baptiste Montini to the Petrine ministry. In addition to those items on his agenda, the new pontiff's eyes will be drawn to a number of warning lights blinking on the Church's dashboard. They are alerting him to the areas where evangelization is losing steam.

In Europe, traditionally Catholic strongholds like Poland, Italy, and even Spain have seen the numbers of the faithful eroded by secularism. Nevertheless, these European churches have recently been showing an upswing in vitality and enthusiasm, particularly among young people.

In Africa, Catholicism has undergone phenomenal expansion. In 2009, there were 179 million Catholics there; by 2050, the number is expected to be 320 million. Africa is also the continent with the fastest-growing number of priests and seminarians. Fifty years after the Second Vatican Council, Benedict XVI declared that Africa "represents an enormous spiritual 'lung' for humanity," referring to the number of laity involved in pastoral action. But this Catholic dynamic is getting stiff competition from Islam. And the African church has also been weakened by scandals, such as corruption and political compromise in the Ivory Coast, and moral affairs involving clergy. Benedict had encouraged a "clean hands" operation that needs to be pursued.

During the African Synod of 2009, other subjects of concern were raised: political crises and civil wars; increasing poverty and issues related to migration; competition from Islam, evangelical churches, and fundamentalist sects that thrive on growing destitution.

Asia seems to be promising terrain for Catholicism. The number of Catholics is on the rise, but in many countries Catholicism is still seen as a foreign religion imported from the West. Nevertheless, Catholics represent the majority of the population in the Philippines (87 percent of some 95 million inhabitants). The Church commands great respect there, as it is seen as a moral compass in a society shaken by corruption and a tense political and social situation.

In East Timor, Catholics represent 90 percent of a population of over a million people. The Church played an important role there in the years leading up to independence from Indonesia. On the other hand, Catholics are a minority in India, where they have to strike a delicate balance with their Hindu and Muslim countrymen. Nevertheless, Catholic schools and hospitals are enjoyed by all! In Vietnam, despite the Communist Party's hold on the country, vocations are flourishing.

The Catholic Church in Asia is still deeply marked by the Western tradition, and the last Council seems to have practically passed it by. Tremendous progress still needs to be made in inculturation. Interfaith dialogue is not at all common, not even with the Buddhists, who dominate in this part of the world. Yet both Christians and Buddhists are subjected to the same religious repression in the last Communist bastions (China, North Korea, Laos, and Vietnam).

In **North America**, after the crisis caused by pedophile priests that shook the episcopate to its foundations and laid some dioceses low, the goal now is to rebuild confidence and to start looking forward once again. Although American society is still strongly religious, atheism and individualism are on the rise. Catholicism's recent growth in North America is largely due to immigration — essentially thanks to Hispanic immigration to the United States and Asian immigration to Canada.

In **South America**, the new pope's continent of origin, the Church still exerts a powerful influence. Representing

40 percent of the worldwide Catholic population, Latin America has been the most important Catholic continent since the 1980s. But evangelical and Pentecostal churches have been catching on in working-class areas, to the detriment of Catholicism, which was weakened by the liberation theology controversies that shook the continent during the 1980s. To counter this, the South American church is counting on the enthusiasm of charismatic groups, as well as on a new generation of priests. In Brazil, for instance, which is the single largest Catholic country in the world, sacerdotal vocations are on the rise. Nevertheless, at the same time, religious practice has suffered a significant drop. Politically speaking, the Church needs to deal with the weakening of the state and the deepening inequality that is causing mafias to expand. South America is also the continent where the greatest number of priests have been assassinated. In Venezuela, Argentina, and Mexico, the Church is seen as a bastion of opposition to the government.

Pope Francis will have an opportunity to address these challenges on the spot in August 2013, when he goes to the World Youth Days, in Rio de Janeiro. Latin America will surely reserve a triumphant welcome for "their pope." And he will seize the occasion to address young people, perhaps urging the "Francis generation" to rise up and become advance scouts for that evangelization he was hoping would occupy the streets and squares of Buenos Aires, reaching out to all and sundry.

A New Style of Papacy

"The style is the man," as Georges-Louis Leclerc de Buffon, an eighteenth-century French naturalist, famously said. In this sense, Pope Francis wasted no time in overturning entrenched Vatican custom by keeping and even asserting his own, no-frills style: a simple man with an easy, spontaneous connection to people. After Joseph Ratzinger's discreet, intellectual pontificate, the one inaugurated by Jorge Mario Bergoglio struck an entirely different note, marking a clear change. The two men are fundamentally different. While both come from humble backgrounds, their experiences are quite divergent.

Ratzinger was shaped by his long experience as a university professor, and by a temperament that led him to seek solitude, to prefer reading and writing in a quiet study or library. Bergoglio, on the other hand, a sincere, although discreet, person, has always enjoyed reaching out to people, and is always eager to start a dialogue. One is a man of ideas and meditative thought, the other is more open to others and to action. But they both enjoy an intense spiritual life steeped in prayer and are attracted to monastic life. Who knows? Perhaps Pope Francis will enjoy going for a stroll with his predecessor in the Vatican's conventual cloister where he now lives in monk-like reclusion.

In any case, Benedict's resignation will make it easier for his successor to adjust the office to appear less monarchic, and more human and accessible. One could say that by choosing to abandon his Petrine ministry, Benedict actually freed his successor of a certain number of constraints and taboos that hitherto had prevented popes from being more themselves. So a radically new papacy is there for the inventing, thanks to successive initiatives of the departing and the arriving pontiffs. What's more, by taking the name Francis, the new bishop of Rome has given a kind of pledge to those — both within the Church and outside it — who long to see the Vatican present itself in a way that is in greater conformance with the simplicity, humility, and poverty that the gospel elevates to the role of paths to heaven on earth.

Relations with Beijing

Asia is the continent of the future. For the Catholic Church, which is keeping a close eye on it, Asia represents more than a billion Chinese to evangelize. For now, the Catholic community in China represents only a tiny minority of the country's total population. And their situation is extremely awkward. First of all, they live under close surveillance by the Chinese Communist Party, which has a firm hold on power. And second, since 1957 the community has been divided into two. One part belongs to the so-called patriotic church, which is controlled by the Communist Party: that church's bishops are ordained without the See of Peter's approval. The other part is a clandestine church, which is loyal to Rome but is persecuted by the Communist regime. Some ties do exist between the two communities, however, and there has been a "growing rapprochement" between Beijing and the Holy See over the past few years.

But the Chinese regime is fickle, changing its attitude periodically, increasing or relieving pressure on the clandestine church depending on the circumstances or its interests at the time. For Rome, the task is a tricky one. It must protect the religious freedom of the faithful, work toward reunification of the two Chinese Catholic churches — within the scope of loyalty and fidelity to the pope — provide for theological and pastoral formation for Catholic communities, and gird the faithful against the temptations of consumerism.

In May 2007, Benedict XVI wrote an open letter to the Catholic Church in China in which he urged the clandestine and patriotic churches to come together. The 2008 Beijing Olympics and the 2010 World's Fair in Shanghai prompted the Chinese government to allow episcopal consecrations within the state-sanctioned church that had first been approved by the Vatican. But in November 2010, Beijing changed its mind and imposed the ordination of a bishop who had been rejected by the Holy See. In 2011, Rome excommunicated several bishops who had been consecrated without the Vatican's authorization. Beijing retaliated by arresting priests of the clandestine church. Each of the adversaries cautiously advanced its pawns in this ongoing chess match: when Beijing urged the Vatican to break off diplomatic relations with Taiwan, the pope, not wishing to be intimidated, appointed a Salesian from Hong Kong to the

position of Secretary of the Congregation for the Evangelization of Peoples, thereby reaffirming that the Chinese
church belongs to the Catholic Church.

The Lefebvrian Quarrel

Resolving the schism created in 1988 by Monsignor Marcel
Lefebvre — the leader of the fundamentalist opposition to
the Second Vatican Council — was one of the preceding
pontiff's utmost priorities. It must be admitted that Benedict XVI failed to win back into the fold of the Roman Catholic Church much of the flock that had strayed to the Society of St. Pius X (SSPX). Despite the efforts made — lifting
the excommunications of the four schismatic bishops and
broadening the use of the Tridentine (Latin) Mass — and
despite the offer to grant SSPX canonical status comparable
to Opus Dei's, Monsignor Fellay's fundamentalist Catholics
didn't deign to sign the agreement protocol that was submit-
ted to them by Rome.

It is as though the fundamentalists were entrenched in
deliberate, intransigent opposition to the very principles of
the Second Vatican Council: religious freedom, ecumenism, and interfaith dialogue. Since negotiations between the
SSPX and the Congregation for the Doctrine of the Faith
have broken down, one can't help but wonder if Pope Francis
is going to try to kick-start them again or, on the contrary, to
let the matter ride for a while.

If truth be told, this whole business had been poisoned from the outset by the English bishop Richard Williamson's 2009 negative statements. The outcry they caused certainly didn't make things any easier for Benedict. All the less so in that his reaching out to the fundamentalists was never really understood by a broad swath of the public, who suspected him of wanting to restore pre–Vatican II liturgical forms or even to dispense with the teachings of Vatican II entirely. It will be interesting to see what judgment a New World pope will bring to bear on this thorny business, which has such deep European roots.

Interfaith Dialogue

John Paul II was the great promoter of interfaith dialogue. He invited the most influential religious leaders from around the planet to Assisi in 1986 for a day of prayer for peace. He was the first pope to enter a synagogue and a mosque. And in 2000, Christianity's jubilee year, he did acts of penance for all the faults committed by those who called themselves Christians throughout history — from the Inquisition to contemporary anti-Semitism. Before the *Kotel,* or Wailing Wall, in Jerusalem, John Paul sought forgiveness for the persecutions committed in the name of Christian anti-Semitism.

His successor, Benedict XVI, was at first somewhat reticent about "relativism," which he feared might lead to interfaith events focusing on points of convergence, to the detriment of points of divergence. In 2006 Benedict gave a Conference on Faith and Reason at the University of Regensburg that provoked a heated reaction in Muslim countries. The crisis peaked with the suspension of relations between the Holy See and the Grand Imam of the Egyptian Muslim University of Al-Azhar, the highest authority in the Sunni Muslim world. Things calmed down after the pope's successful visit to Turkey. Benedict believed theological dialogue between religions was bound to fail. Therefore he promised a "cultural" approach to interfaith relations, particularly with Islam, in which true believers could base mutual understanding on a foundation of shared values.

His relationship with Judaism was smoother and more cordial than that with Islam except for two occasions: when Pope Benedict rehabilitated the Good Friday prayer for the conversion of Jews from the traditional, 1962 edition of the missal, and again when the question of the beatification of Pius XII, whose attitude during World War II has led to great controversy and debate both among historians and within the Jewish community, was raised once again. It will be up to Pope Francis to make his own mark on dialogue between the religions, and to clearly state his position on Islam, a religion whose presence is more discreet and its growth slower in Latin America than elsewhere.

Redefining Ecumenism

After having been an "ardent obligation" of the Second Vatican Council, ecumenism has fallen by the wayside somewhat. All those years of dialogue don't seem to have produced much in the way of tangible results. Except perhaps at the Community of Taizé, in Burgundy, France, where the hundred-plus members of an ecumenical monastic order founded by Brother Roger Schütz continue to share their passion for unity with the 100,000 or so young Europeans that visit them each year.

Aware of the impasse into which ecumenical efforts had fallen, Benedict XVI redirected them toward a more global objective: resisting the cultural relativism that seems to be part of the zeitgeist. The other goal is less concerned with dialogue than it is with preparing for a return to Church unity through concrete initiatives. The ordinariate created for the three Anglican bishops who wanted to join the Catholic Church is a reflection of this pragmatic, moderate, and patient ecumenical vision.

Dialogue with the Orthodox world was started up again at the initiative of Benedict. But it is difficult because of friction between the patriarchates of Moscow and Constantinople, which exacerbates their divergences in terms of primacy and the organization of diasporas. During the preceding pontificate, relations between the Catholic Church and the Patriarchate of Moscow were strengthened. Although they are still divided over issues of power, there has been great rapprochement over moral issues.

The principal obstacle to ecumenical progress is the rebirth, over the past twenty years, of "Uniate" Catholic churches, that is, those that are "united to" or in full communion with Rome. A not insignificant number of Russians, Ukrainians, and Romanians of Orthodox descent are attracted to these churches, which they see as being more independent from political power and more open to modernity. Moscow has criticized Rome for its proselytizing and its lack of consultation when founding bishoprics in traditionally Orthodox areas!

In 2017, Christians will have the chance to start the long march back toward unity when Lutherans in particular and all of Protestantism celebrate the 500th anniversary of the start of the Reformation. It will surely be up to Pope Francis to take steps to revive and bring greater visibility to ecumenism, which hopes to overcome the outrage and countertestimonial that the divisions of the Christian community — which comprises more than 2 billion believers around the world — represent.

Violence against Christians

The Vatican is deeply concerned about the fate of Christian minorities in the Muslim world and about the future of Middle Eastern Christianity. Some 13 million Christians live in the Middle East, including Turkey and Iran. But considering the economic and political difficulties they have to face, as well as the rise of Islamic fundamentalism and the various conflicts that have caused such upheaval in the region, many of them have been choosing to emigrate to Europe, North America, and Australia, so this figure is constantly falling. Half of the 500,000 Christians who lived in Iraq before the Anglo-American invasion of 2003 have since gone into exile.

In Syria, where a civil war has been raging for two years now, Christians represent 10 percent of the population. They find themselves in a complex situation, caught between a regime that has lost its legitimacy and a rebellion that includes *jihadi* militants. Nevertheless, there are several Christian militants in the Syrian National Council in exile. They want to prove their desire to participate in change once Bashar al-Assad's regime finally falls. Hopefully, their involvement and commitment to defending Syrian Christians' rights will help prevent a mass exodus like the one of Christians from Iraq.

The Catholic Church demands freedom of religion wherever building churches or practicing religion is banned or harshly restricted. In Pakistan, for example, so-called blasphemy laws have caused persecution. To help stabilize Christian populations in the East whose welfare has been threatened by the region's conflicts and civil wars, the Vatican defends not only specific rights, but also the idea of equal citizenship for all.

In October 2010, the Synod of Middle Eastern Bishops expressed its profound concern for the future, or even the survival, of their communities, which are divided into various rites (Syrian, Coptic, Armenian, Chaldean, Byzantine, Maronite, and more) that are poorly connected even to each other. Throughout his pontificate, Benedict XVI never ceased drawing international attention to the welfare of these communities, which have been repeatedly threatened and even attacked. The synod that he convened underscored the need to teach these Christians, who are often marked by an extremely traditional faith, to enter into a confident dialogue with Muslims. During a significant visit to Lebanon in September 2012, Benedict reiterated his appeal in favor of harmonious cohabitation between Christians and Muslims in the region: "May we, with God's help, be converted so as to work ardently to establish the peace that is necessary for harmonious coexistence among brothers," he said, adding, "whatever their origins and religious convictions," insisting yet again on the central message of his visit: the peaceful coexistence of Christians and Muslims in a Middle Eastern society that recognizes the plurality of religious traditions.

"The persecution of Christians is the primary emergency in the world in terms of violence. No other faith is under such attack," declared Massimo Introvigne in the French newspaper *La Croix* on March 14, 2013. Introvigne is the director of the Center for Studies on New Religions (CESNUR) and the coordinator of the Observatory of Religious Freedom for the Italian Ministry of Foreign Affairs. According to him, 105,000 Christians — of all denominations — were murdered in 2012. And 10 percent of the 2 billion Christians in the world —

meaning some 200 million people — were persecuted because of their faith, mainly in Africa and Asia. Murderously violent acts were committed in the name of Islam (by the Boko Haram sect in Nigeria, the Sunni fundamentalist movement Jamaat-e-Islam in Pakistan, and as reprisals against the West in Egypt and Iraq) and of Hinduism (by the Rashtriya Swayamsevak Sangh [RSS] in India, at the instigation of the nationalist BJP). Violence can also derive from clashes between ethnic groups (in the Democratic Republic of the Congo) or between tribal groups opposing Christians and Muslims (as in the Sudan and Ethiopia).

Liberalization of Morals

Not a single European country has been spared by secularization, some more affected than others. Ireland was traumatized by criminal sexual abuse cases involving priests and bishops. Austria faced massive upheaval from within the Church itself: 400 priests signed a "Call to Disobedience" warning their hierarchy that they would give Holy Communion to remarried divorcées. In Germany too, discontent is growing. In 2011, hundreds of priests and deacons signed a petition demanding access to the Eucharist for remarried divorcées. This subject is extremely divisive and was raised repeatedly at local councils throughout western Europe. During the pontificate of Benedict XVI, it was just one of many issues that caused some of the faithful to leave the Church

— others include scandals like those involving pedophile priests, the Williamson affair, and Vatileaks. In 2011, more than 126,000 people formally left the Church. This defection is reflected in the drop in the number of baptisms and weddings and vocations, and of course in church finances!

At the same time, major ethical upheavals have been causing debate throughout the Western world over homosexuality, euthanasia, embryonic research, etc. In France, the Church has been at the forefront of the fight against the legalization of same-sex marriage, which Parliament passed in late April 2013, but which has yet to be approved by the Constitutional Council. And it will soon be opposing partisans of assisted suicide. In the United States, Church leadership has been engaged in a tug-of-war with the Obama administration over the birth-control mandate in the health-care plan that would oblige dioceses to reimburse contraception, abortion pills, and sterilization for their lay employees. Benedict XVI set the tone in this fight against the concrete effects of secularism and relativism. His successor, who attracted attention as the leader in the fight against same-sex marriage in Argentina, will not stray from Benedict's path. He may well lean on the analyses of his predecessor, with whom he shares convictions about the fundamentals, then draw on his own personal experience to find ways to convince the Western world, which has been turning its back on Christian values more and more. But as an open-minded man of dialogue, Pope Francis will also be careful not to let his defense of evangelical ideals enlarge the gulf that has formed between the dominant modern culture and the Catholic Church.

The Worldwide Economic Crisis

The economic crisis creates an opportunity for the Church to come to the aid of those who have suffered the most: households that are deeply in debt, unemployed youth, the isolated elderly, and outcasts and illegal aliens. For this purpose, the Church has parish-based networks and movements as well as charitable organizations. In many regions of the world that have been confronted with the crisis since 2008, and with endemic poverty for even longer, the Catholic Church is one of the pillars of active solidarity. Through the voice of Catholic universities and Justice and Peace Commissions, it has repeatedly denounced the excesses of unbridled financial capitalism and contributes both to think tanks and to the training of economic experts, and executives and leaders of firms and companies committed to social justice and shared wealth.

The new pope Francis, who distinguished himself in his native country by assailing the excesses of unbridled liberal and financial capitalism, will undoubtedly be equally combative against a globalization that recognizes no other values than financial ones and denies the cultural and historical realities that have been Catholicism's for centuries. How will the New World pope advise Catholics to look upon the crisis and its "castaways"? Surely with the same gaze he described as archbishop of Buenos Aires in 2011: "The greatest exclusion consists in not even 'seeing' the outcast — those who sleep in the streets and aren't seen as people but as part of the filth and abandon of the urban landscape, or our culture of waste, of the 'dump' — the human city grows in the gaze that truly 'sees' fellow citizens in those others. In this way, a gaze of faith is the ferment of a socially responsible gaze."

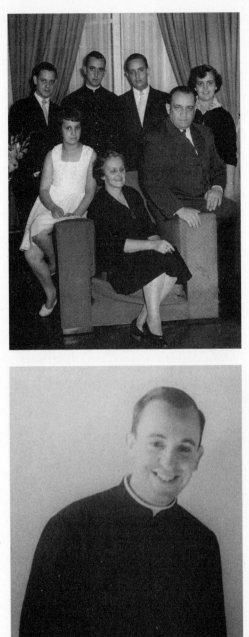

Jorge Mario Bergoglio (back row, second from left), his parents, Maria Regina and José Mario Francisco, and his brothers and sisters.

As a young priest, in 1973.

Right: As a young priest, preaching at Mass.

Below: The Argentinean cardinal celebrating the washing of the feet on Maundy Thursday (March 2008) at the Hogar de Cristo Care Center for People with Substance Addictions, in Buenos Aires.

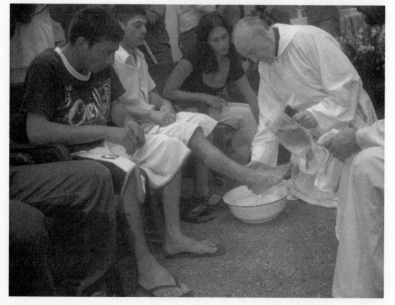

In the subway in Buenos Aires, on May 28, 2008.

Embracing Pope John Paul II when he made Jorge Mario Bergoglio cardinal on July 21, 2001.

On Saint Peter's Square in Rome. Bergoglio was a member of both a pontifical commission and a pontifical council. Here he is heading to the Curia, on March 3, 2013.

A historic gesture: for his first public appearance, on March
13, 2013, Pope Francis asks the faithful to pray for God's
blessing for him. © AFP/VINCENZO PINTO

The first pontifical blessing, on March 13, 2013, as the 266th Roman pontiff, successor to Peter, the Prince of Apostles. © AFP/GIUSEPPE CACACE

The newly elected Pope Francis warmly greets the people of his diocese of Rome, calling upon their brotherhood. © AFP/OSSERVATORE ROMANO

CHAPTER III

Pope Francis in His Own Words

The surprise of Benedict XVI's resignation, followed by the unexpected election of Pope Francis, means that the latter's writings are not yet readily accessible to the English-speaking public. Unlike his predecessor — who was well known prior to his accession to the See of Peter as one of the great Catholic scholars of the twentieth century, and whose work had been largely translated and published around the world — as an author, Pope Francis remains to be discovered.

As we wait for publishers to get a chance to offer readers his principal writings, here is a first look at some of the new pontiff's most significant speeches and texts, to allow us to get to know the character of a man who is fairly discreet but who knows how to observe the world with a sharp eye.

In a World of Castaways

In May 1995, Monsignor Jorge Mario Bergoglio addressed the entire community of the Jesuit University del Salvador in Buenos

Aires. Going beyond the specific circumstance, he shared his complex but fascinating reasoning about contemporary beliefs.

He referred to postmodernism and to the self-questioning required of a university in order to find and give meaning to an identity that goes beyond the ambiguities specific to the contemporary crisis.

In those days of March 1975, what Father Arrupe had requested of the Argentine provincial of the Society of Jesus on July 12, 1973, was finally taking place: the refounding of the University del Salvador. "Refounding" in the etymological sense: going back to that which founds it, going back to the powerful inspiration and will to construct of those who pioneered this project. In those days, we often referred to the "fundamental mystery." So many memories! Twenty years have passed. . . .

. . . I propose a rereading through the prism of memory of "History and Change," of its guiding principles: the struggle against atheism, progress via a return to our roots, universality through difference. . . .

When I wrote the Charter of Principles, lo these twenty years ago, we had no idea of the course history would take. We were living in an era of scientism and utilitarianism, an era of clear and systematic ideologies and systems. Today, however, the powerful structures of modernism are irremediably weakened, and what is left of the shipwreck (which we share) we call, with a certain intellectual modesty, "postmodernism." The historical challenge holds all the ambiguity of a crisis, and modern man — from force of habit — tends to rebuild what was there "yesterday," when all that is left on the beaches are the remnants of an incomplete journey. So let us not be surprised if, in the gallery of today's world, we find strange combinations coexisting: racial or tribal hatred with preachers of peace and harmony with the cosmos; those who worship computers and the cyber-world and modern "yogis" of transcendental meditation; frantic searching for a better quality of life while an ever-increasing number of inhabitants of the world are sinking into poverty, and still others are dying of hunger. This entire panorama appears to be wrapped in a tendency on the part of governments and the powerful to rationalize their decisions by avoiding major conflicts while channeling the prices and contradictions of major changes toward communities, ethnicities, and sectors that have been marginalized by various societies.

We are part of this new situation, this shipwreck: we are among the castaways; and we too may well try to rebuild out of force of habit, with the tools of a ship that no longer exists. Or, on the contrary, to deny our uncertainty by inhibiting the creative force of our own history, our memory history. Castaways are always alone with themselves and their own history, which is their greatest wealth. So today we are asking that memory to come to our aid. We do not ask it of simplistic repetition nor of the pitiful snobbery of those who thoughtlessly accommodate to their era; we ask it of this memory that is a veritable anamnesis, true reunion.

Like the prophet Elijah, who withdrew to listen in silence to the breeze of the Spirit; like in the celebration of the Eucharist, when with our own bodies and those of our brothers we meet in the body of Christ. As a place of endless searching for wisdom, the walls of this university encircle the perfect space for this exercise in memory: finding ourselves within the principles that allow us to take our vows, unblocking what keeps us from going forward, staying true, as well, to our mission, which is precisely what we wished and which is now and must remain so. How can we remember these principles when faced with new challenges? Where shall we look for the path that will set the castaways back in the right direction? Let us come back now to the Charter of Principles and retrace the three guiding lines (the fight against atheism, progress via a return to our roots, universality through difference) and attempt to reread it with greater discernment.

The fight against atheism. Until recently, the influence of skeptical atheism and the lack of a transcendent vision of history and of life were a constant preoccupation. Our consecration to God the Father based on a view of the world that is implied by the fact of springing from the bosom of the Mystical Body of the Verb Incarnate, and particularly from the life experience of the faithful, the true believers, has clearly placed us in our own position of foundation and identity from which to face down our adversaries. Resistance to systems or schools of thought and ideologies that would deny that faith can create culture leads us to rethink, and to create our own formulations, especially when the thinking is motivated by the negation of the Absolute or of God's own person (this may well be one of the causes of the deterioration of modernism). Those militants who boasted of their atheism or their scientism faced us with untroubled brows, opposed us in new ways. But nowadays, on the other hand, we are living with a worried humanity, one that is looking for meaning in its own existence, desiring to articulate languages and discourses to reconstruct the harmony of lost knowledge; we live with a humanity that is anxious to compose its "ego" in the face of insecurity. We cannot not see this new search for the spiritual as a sign from the Spirit of God.

Yet out of what has been produced by the confusion of crisis, we want to rebuild the vestiges of a wrecked ship: each of us would re-create a divinity depending on if our own powerlessness leaves his wounds or his distress more exposed. This is not the manifestation of Someone who unveils *(apocalupzein)* and reveals *(epiphanein)* himself, but of divinity considered as a revitalizing energy in response to our need to feel welcomed and soothed. Until even the "ego" itself can manage to become aware of its own capacities and — by healing itself of its negative attitudes — discover the essence of love, of divinity. One can, in harmony with the cosmos and nature, prevent and even cure disease (the heart of the miracle) . . . and we could go on enumerating the situations and phenomena of this new religiosity. The point is not to deny the wealth that extremely old cultures can bring, nor the progress of scientific discoveries, nor the strength of affection, but to gird ourselves against the unnatural blend with which we camouflage, yet again, our own disorientation.

On the other hand, we can encounter legions of fanatics who, clinging to their conscious or unconscious fears, wave the flag for gods who justify their aberrant ideas or simply their prejudices and ideologies. That is how, from fundamentalisms of all sorts to New Age ideas — via the mediocrities in our own lives of faith — we have nourished the postmodern castaways from the well-stocked pantry of the religious market. But let us make no mistake: here, yet again, we are building a house with the remnants of old ideologies and esoteric scientisms, or simply by resorting to our bourgeois consumer spirit. The outcome is theism: an Olympus of gods made in our "image and resemblance" in the mirror of our dissatisfactions, our fears, and our self-sufficiencies; gods caught in the trap of their own insecurities, reduced to simple supports or justifications for our illusions and beliefs. A theism that often, in order to explain itself, uses elements of Christianity — not to support but to demolish Christianity by diluting it in the mists of a divinity sprayed over the marketplace.

In a way, we are like the first Church, with the God of Jesus Christ delving into a world in which men are fighting for their own divinity, but in a secularized life. Holding on to the memory of our forefathers in faith can provide a useful analogical vision for helping us find ourselves with the Spirit in our mission, even if the world has changed. Like those first Christians, we should announce, not only with our convincing messages, but above all with our lives, that the Truth founded on the love of Jesus Christ for his Church (i.e., for all those who believe in him) is truly worthy of belief. Because the new atheism is precisely that confusion between gods and men in which no words inspire confidence. Exhausted by messages, we run the risk of falling into incertitude and erroneous indifference, those diseases of the spirit. Today, more than ever, sainthood is a journey: meaning that we must be truthful witnesses to what we believe in and what we love. Which is quite simply crucifying. The gospel, which is Christ, is passed on less by reasoning than by life itself . . . which is a transformed and transformative mirror, a reflection not only of our own opacities but of the World of God. This life of bearing witness can be more than just an example to follow; it can truly be a symbolic fulfillment of a desire tied to the desire of the one whom we cannot explain but in whom we live, because we have allowed ourselves to meet him and because we love him. And we know full well that the symbol creates the culture.

This *métanoia,* this creative conversion, must take place within the very experience of the educative Christian community that we form. In our criteria, in our methods, and in our unceasing search for truth — which does not pretend to be all-powerful, but was instead crucified — we must give this mysterious Christian deed that stems from every true encounter with Jesus Christ: the truth is all the more resplendent for its limitations than for its pretensions. More than just a university that provides enlightenment or that cultivates enlightened schools of thought (which we must never cease seeking and working toward), we must be a community with a taste for delving into Truth and Beauty, a community that enthusiastically invites us to live Goodness. In addition, it is in the silence of study, in the humbleness of sharing and mutual assistance, that we will find the remedy for the mediocrity that leads to corruption and for loss of interest, the two ills that provoke so much incertitude among our youth, which encourages them to escapism and superficiality. The very life of our people who are true believers depends on it, those who anonymously preach the crucified Christ in his suffering and who preach him resuscitated in hope and in simple, unsophisticated joys. It is this people that, in our Charter of Principles, we seek to imitate. I hope that we will never cease drawing inspiration from their suffering faces, their vulnerability and anguish — which we know well in today's Argentina — in order to urge us to seek, study, and create even more. When, in the streets, we encounter the wandering homeless, the abandoned, the children who beg or steal because they are poor, the young people who are lost to drugs and alcohol, the workers who suffer from lack of money and from insecurity on a daily basis . . . when we see the lines of people waiting patiently at hospitals who come back day after day . . . then there is no doubt: God is there; Christ, from his cross, from his limitation, is calling to us to go further every day. Against the diluted theism that all-powerful postmodernism offers us, we continue to assert that "the Word was made flesh" . . . and we know that he who denies this is the Deceiver and the Antichrist (cf. 2 John 1:7). This is not — as it was twenty years ago — the negation of God, this is a caricature of him: this miserable transcendence that isn't even sufficient to deal with the limits of immanence, simply because it doesn't invite us to reach any human limitation or to lay our hand on any wound (if it did, it could say, like Thomas, "My Lord and my God"). Today, our fight against atheism is called the fight against theism. And today also, the truth that Malègue [a French Catholic novelist and theologian], in a different cultural context but in reference to the same reality, stated so wisely in the early twentieth century is the rule: "It is not God who is incomprehensible for me if He is Christ, it is God who is strange for me if He is not Christ." In the light of this affirmation of God made manifest in the flesh of Christ, we can define the task of formation and research within the university: facing reality with the true paschal spirit is a reflection of Christian hope. Crucified humanity does not give us a reason to invent gods or to think ourselves all-powerful: much more than that — through creative work and our own spiritual development — it is an invitation to believe and to make manifest a new experience of the resurrection, of new life.

(Excerpt from Jorge Mario Bergoglio, S.J., *Twenty Years Later: A Reading through the Prism of Memory of the Document "History and Change"* [Buenos Aires: Del Salvador University, May 17, 1995], pp. 9-18.)

Prayer and Sacrifice

When the Argentinean government decided in 2010 to legalize same-sex marriage, Monsignor Bergoglio seemed to be one of the main opponents to this law, at the price of an intense conflict with the government, incarnated by Cristina Kirchner, the president. Realizing how difficult it would be to defend the cause of traditional family values, the archbishop of Buenos Aires didn't hesitate to ask for help, and above all, prayers of intercession, from the contemplative communities of his diocese.

Letter from Cardinal Bergoglio
to the Carmelite nuns of his diocese.

Buenos Aires, June 22, 2010

My Dear Sisters,

I am writing these few lines to each of you who are in the four monasteries of Buenos Aires. Over the next few weeks, the Argentinean people must confront a situation whose outcome could gravely harm the family.

The issue is proposed legislation that would allow persons of the same sex to marry. What is at stake here are the identity and survival of families: father, mother, children. What is at stake are the lives of numerous children who will be discriminated against beforehand and deprived of the human maturity that God willed them to have, with a father and a mother. What is at stake is a clear rejection of God's law, which is engraved in our hearts as well.

I recall the words of Saint Teresa of the Child Jesus as she spoke of the infirmity of her childhood. She said that the devil's jealousy sought revenge on her family after her older sister joined the Carmel. Here, too, is jealousy of the devil, through which sin came into the world: jealousy that deceitfully tries to destroy God's image, which is man and woman who receive the commandment to be fruitful and to multiply, and to govern the earth. Let us not be naïve: this is not just a political battle, but an attempt to destroy God's plan. This is not just a proposed law (which is just a tool), but a "maneuver" by the father of all lies who is seeking to sow confusion and to deceive the children of God. And Jesus said that to defend ourselves from this lying accuser, he would send us the Spirit of Truth.

Today, in this situation, our country needs the special assistance of the Holy Spirit, which shines the light of truth in the midst of the shadows of error. It needs this Advocate to defend us from the many sophisms with which they are trying at all costs to justify this proposed law, and which confuse and deceive even people of good will.

And that is why I am calling upon you and asking you for prayers and sacrifice, Saint Teresa's two invincible weapons. Cry out to the Lord that he may send his spirit to the senators who have said they will vote. That they not do it under the sway of error or contingent circumstances, but according to what natural law and God's law show them. Pray for them and their families. That God may visit them, strengthen them, and comfort them. Pray that the senators do great good for our nation.

This bill will be discussed in the Senate after July 13. Let us look to Saint Joseph, Mary, and the Child Jesus, and let us fervently ask them to defend the Argentinean family in its time of need. Let us recall what God himself told his people in a time of great anguish: "This war is not yours, but God's." That they may succor, defend, and accompany us in this war of God.

Thank you for what you will do in this struggle for the nation. And, please, I beg you, pray also for me. May Jesus bless you, and may the Blessed Virgin protect you.

Affectionately,

Jorge Mario Bergoglio, S.J.
Archbishop of Buenos Aires
In Cordibus Jesu et Mariae

I Ask You to Pray to the Lord That He Will Bless Me

The first message from Pope Francis on Saint Peter's balcony. By their simplicity, his first words conquered Rome, the Church, and men and women around the world.

Brothers and sisters, good evening!

You know that it was the duty of the Conclave to give Rome a Bishop. It seems that my brother Cardinals have gone to the ends of the earth to get one . . . but here we are. . . . I thank you for your welcome. The diocesan community of Rome now has its Bishop. Thank you! And first of all, I would like to offer a prayer for our Bishop Emeritus, Benedict XVI. Let us pray together for him, that the Lord may bless him and that Our Lady may keep him.

[Our Father, Hail Mary, Glory Be . . .]

And now, we take up this journey: Bishop and People. This journey of the Church of Rome which presides in charity over all the Churches. A journey of fraternity, of love, of trust among us. Let us always pray for one another. Let us pray for the whole world, that there may be a great spirit of fraternity. It is my hope for you that this journey of the Church, which we start today, and in which my Cardinal Vicar, here present, will assist me, will be fruitful for the evangelization of this most beautiful city.

And now I would like to give the blessing, but first — first I ask a favour of you: before the Bishop blesses his people, I ask you to pray to the Lord that he will bless me: the prayer of the people asking the blessing for their Bishop. Let us make, in silence, this prayer: your prayer over me.

[. . .]

Now I will give the Blessing to you and to the whole world, to all men and women of good will.

[Blessing]

Brothers and sisters, I leave you now. Thank you for your welcome. Pray for me and until we meet again. We will see each other soon. Tomorrow I wish to go and pray to Our Lady, that she may watch over all of Rome. Good night and sleep well!

(Translation from www.vatican.va.)

Going Straight to the Heart of Matters

His first homily before the cardinals gathered in the Sistine Chapel.

In these three readings, I see a common element: that of movement. In the first reading, it is the movement of a journey; in the second reading, the movement of building the Church; in the third, in the Gospel, the movement involved in professing the faith. Journeying, building, professing.

Journeying. "O House of Jacob, come, let us walk in the light of the Lord" (*Is* 2:5). This is the first thing that God said to Abraham: Walk in my presence and live blamelessly. Journeying: our life is a journey, and when we stop moving, things go wrong. Always journeying, in the presence of the Lord, in the light of the Lord, seeking to live with the blamelessness that God asked of Abraham in his promise.

Building. Building the Church. We speak of stones: stones are solid; but living stones, stones anointed by the Holy Spirit. Building the Church, the Bride of Christ, on the cornerstone that is the Lord himself. This is another kind of movement in our lives: building.

Thirdly, professing. We can walk as much as we want, we can build many things, but if we do not profess Jesus Christ, things go wrong. We may become a charitable NGO, but not the Church, the Bride of the Lord. When we are not walking, we stop moving. When we are not building on the stones, what happens? The same thing that happens to children on the beach when they build sandcastles: everything is swept away, there is no solidity. When we do not profess Jesus Christ, the saying of Léon Bloy comes to mind: "Anyone who does not pray to the Lord prays to the devil." When we do not profess Jesus Christ, we profess the worldliness of the devil, a demonic worldliness.

Journeying, building, professing. But things are not so straightforward, because in journeying, building, professing, there can sometimes be jolts, movements that are not properly part of the journey: movements that pull us back.

This Gospel continues with a situation of a particular kind. The same Peter who professed Jesus Christ, now says to him: You are the Christ, the Son of the living God. I will follow you, but let us not speak of the Cross. That has nothing to do with it. I will follow you on other terms, but without the Cross. When we journey without the Cross, when we build without the Cross, when we profess Christ without the

69

Cross, we are not disciples of the Lord, we are worldly: we may be bishops, priests, cardinals, popes, but not disciples of the Lord.

My wish is that all of us, after these days of grace, will have the courage, yes, the courage, to walk in the presence of the Lord, with the Lord's Cross; to build the Church on the Lord's blood which was poured out on the Cross; and to profess the one glory: Christ crucified. And in this way, the Church will go forward.

My prayer for all of us is that the Holy Spirit, through the intercession of the Blessed Virgin Mary, our Mother, will grant us this grace: to walk, to build, to profess Jesus Christ crucified. Amen.

(Translation from www.vatican.va.)

"Let Us Not Yield to Pessimism"

There are several different reasons to speak about the devil: to scare people, to manipulate the irrational, or to judge one's peers. But here, Pope Francis, while explicitly naming him, designates him as the source of pessimism and discouragement.

In this way, isn't he agreeing with John XXIII, who denounced the "prophets of misery" several decades ago?

This is what Pope Francis said to the cardinals present in Rome on Friday, March 15, 2013, at 5 P.M. in the Clementine Hall of the Apostolic Palace.

Dear Brother Cardinals,

The period of the conclave has been a momentous time not only for the College of Cardinals, but also for all the faithful. In these days we have felt almost tangibly the affection and the solidarity of the universal Church, as well as the concern of so many people who, even if they do not share our faith, look to the Church and the Holy See with respect and admiration. From every corner of the earth, fervent prayers have been offered up by the Christian people for the new Pope, and my first encounter with the thronging crowd in Saint Peter's Square was deeply moving. With that evocative image of the people gathered in joyful prayer still impressed on my memory, I want to express my sincere thanks to the bishops, priests, consecrated persons, young people, families, and the elderly for their spiritual closeness, so touching and so deeply felt.

I want to express my sincere and profound gratitude to all of you, my dear venerable brother Cardinals, for your ready cooperation in the task of leading the Church during the period of the *Sede Vacante*. I greet each one of you warmly, beginning with the Dean of the College of Cardinals, Cardinal Angelo Sodano, whom I thank for his devoted words and his fervent good wishes addressed to me on behalf of all of you. I also thank Cardinal Tarcisio Bertone, Camerlengo of the Holy Roman Church, for his attentive service during this transitional period, as well as our dear friend Cardinal Giovanni Battista Re, who led us during the conclave: thank you very much! My thoughts turn with particular affection to the Cardinals who, on account of age or ill health, made their contribution and expressed their love for the Church by offering up their sufferings and their prayers. And I must tell you that the day before yesterday, Cardinal Mejia had a heart attack and was taken to Pio XI Hospital. But his condition is described as stable, and he has sent us his greetings.

Nor can I omit to thank all those who carried out various tasks in the preparation and the conduct of the conclave, providing the Cardinals with security and peace of mind in this period of such importance for the life of the Church.

My thoughts turn with great affection and profound gratitude to my venerable Predecessor Benedict XVI, who enriched and invigorated the Church during the years of his Pontificate by his teaching, his goodness, his leadership, his faith, his humility and his meekness. All this remains as a spiritual heritage for us all. The Petrine ministry, lived with total dedication, found in him a wise and humble exponent, his gaze always firmly on Christ, the risen Christ, present and alive in the Eucharist. We will always accompany him with fervent prayers, with constant remembrance, with undying and affectionate gratitude. We feel that Benedict XVI has kindled a flame deep within our hearts: a flame that will continue to burn because it will be fed by his prayers, which continue to sustain the Church on her spiritual and missionary journey.

Dear brother Cardinals, this meeting of ours is intended to be, as it were, a prolongation of the intense ecclesial communion we have experienced during this period. Inspired by a profound sense of responsibility and supported by a great love for Christ and for the Church, we have prayed together, fraternally sharing our feelings, our experiences and reflections. In this atmosphere of great warmth we have come to know one another better in a climate of mutual openness; and this is good, because we are brothers. Someone said to me: the Cardinals are the priests of the Holy Father. That community, that friendship, that closeness will do us all good. And our acquaintance and mutual openness have helped us to be docile to the action of the Holy Spirit. He, the Paraclete, is the ultimate source of every initiative and manifestation of faith. It is a curious thing: it makes me think of this. The Paraclete creates all the differences among the Churches, almost as if he were an Apostle of Babel. But on the other hand, it is he who creates unity from these differences, not in "equality," but in harmony. I remember the Father of the Church who described him thus: *"Ipse harmonia est."* The Paraclete, who gives different charisms to each of us, unites us in this community of the Church, that worships the Father, the Son, and Him, the Holy Spirit.

On the basis of the authentic affective collegiality that unites the College of Cardinals, I express my desire to serve the Gospel with renewed love, helping the Church to become increasingly, in Christ and with Christ, the fruitful vine of the Lord. Inspired also by the celebration of the Year of Faith, all of us together, pastors and members of the faithful, will strive to respond faithfully to the Church's perennial mission: to bring Jesus Christ to mankind and to lead mankind to an encounter with Jesus Christ, the Way, the Truth and the Life, truly present in the Church and also in every person. This meeting leads us to become new men in the mystery of Grace, kindling in the spirit that Christian joy that is the hundredfold given by Christ to those who welcome him into their lives.

As Pope Benedict XVI reminded us so many times in his teachings, and at the end by his courageous and humble gesture, it is Christ who leads the Church through his Spirit. The Holy Spirit is the soul of the Church through his life-giving and unifying force: out of many, he makes one single body, the Mystical Body of Christ. Let us never yield to pessimism, to that bitterness that the devil offers us every day; let us not yield to pessimism or discouragement: let us be quite certain that the Holy Spirit bestows upon the Church, with his powerful breath, the courage to persevere and also to seek new methods of evangelization, so as to bring the Gospel to the uttermost ends of the earth (cf. *Acts* 1:8). Christian truth is attractive and persuasive because it responds to the profound need of human life, proclaiming convincingly that Christ is the one Savior of the whole man and of all men. This proclamation remains as valid today as it was at the origin of Christianity, when the first great missionary expansion of the Gospel took place.

Dear brother Cardinals, take courage! Half of us are advanced in age. Old age is — as I like to say — the seat of life's wisdom. The old have acquired the wisdom that comes from having journeyed through life, like the old man Simeon, the old prophetess Anna in the Temple. And that wisdom enabled them to recognize Jesus. Let us pass on this wisdom to the young: like good wine that improves with age, let us give life's wisdom to the young. I am reminded of a German poet who said of old age: *Es is ruhig, das Alter, und fromm:* it is a time of tranquillity and prayer. And also a time to pass on this wisdom to the young. You will now return to your respective sees to continue your ministry, enriched by the experience of these days, so full of faith and ecclesial communion. This unique and incomparable experience has enabled us to grasp deeply all the beauty of the Church, which is a glimpse of the radiance of the risen Christ: one day we will gaze upon that beautiful face of the risen Christ!

I entrust my ministry and your ministry to the powerful intercession of Mary, our Mother, Mother of the Church. Under her maternal gaze, may each one of you continue gladly along your path, attentive to the voice of her divine Son, strengthening your unity, persevering in your common prayer and bearing witness to the true faith in the constant presence of the Lord. With these sentiments, which I really mean, I impart a heartfelt Apostolic Blessing, which I extend to your co-workers and to all those entrusted to your pastoral care.

(Translation from www.vatican.va.)

Francis from A to T

Abortion: "Once again we see deliberate attempts to limit and suppress the supreme value, which is life, and to ignore the rights of the child waiting to be born. When we talk about a pregnant woman, we are talking about two lives: both of them must be preserved and respected, because life is an absolute value." *(Communiqué, September 10, 2012)*

Bishop: "The bishop is the one who keeps vigil, who cares for hope, while keeping vigil for his people. One spiritual attitude focuses on watching over the flock with an 'over-view': the bishop is in charge of everything that maintains the flock's cohesion. Another spiritual attitude focuses on 'keeping vigil,' on being attentive to dangers. . . . Surveil-lance refers more to paying attention to doctrine and custom, while keeping vigil evokes rather the idea of making sure there is sun and light in people's hearts. Keeping your guard up implies a state of alertness in the face of imminent danger, while keeping vigil implies the patient support of the processes by which the Lord guides his people toward salvation. For surveillance, you need only to be awake, alert, and quick. To keep vigil, you must also have gentleness, patience, and the constancy of lived charity. Surveillance and keeping your guard up speak about the necessity of maintaining control. But keeping vigil speaks to us of hope." *(Speech at the Synod of Bishops, October 2, 2001)*

Buenos Aires: "Buenos Aires looks like a booming city. You can find everything here. But how many exploited children? How many oppressed women? How many brothels? So many things that reek of slavery." *(Homily, December 2008)*

Corruption: "Crimes, tragedies, heavy debts that we have to pay because of corruption. . . . But 'no one's here.' No one takes responsibility for what needs to be done or what has been done. 'No one's here . . .' has become a verity, and perhaps we have become and feel like 'less than nothing.'" *(Homily, May 25 [Argentinean patriotic holiday], 2012)*

Economy: "The imperialism of money clearly displays an idolatrous face. And where there is idolatry, the face of God and the dignity of man, who was created in God's image, are veiled. The new imperialism of money ignores work, through which man's dignity and creativity, which is the image of God's creation, are expressed. But work doesn't interest the speculative economy; it doesn't know what to do with it. That's why it has no problem transforming 30 million workers into unemployed persons." *(Interview in 30 Giorni, January 2002)*

Girlfriend: "I did have one girlfriend. We were part of a group of friends, and we used to go dancing together. Then I discovered my religious vocation." *(Le jésuite, 2010)*

Humility: "Humility reveals the potential trapped inside human smallness. By being aware of both our gifts and our limitations, we free ourselves of the blindness of pride. And just as Jesus praised our Father for the revelation made to the meek, we should also praise our Father for making the May sun rise on those who trust in the gift of freedom, the freedom that grows inside the hearts of a people that wager on greatness without losing sight of their own smallness." *(Homily, May 25, 2011)*

Injustice: "That our Father gives us our daily bread and work is a blessing. Crying out against the injustice that this bread and work are not available to all is part of the blessing. Working with others to share and distribute our bread is another part of the blessing that we ask. This desire and this struggle do our hearts good." *(Homily, August 7, 2012)*

Migrants: "Whoever does not have his heart open to brothers of all races, of all nations, fails in his duty, and his life ends like an unpaid bill, without having honored the existential debt that we all have as individuals. Today, World Day of Migrants and Refugees, let us look at those who were not born in this country. They came here. What a surprise! Like the father or the mother of all of us here. Like my father. They came here for many reasons: to find work, or because of ideological persecution. So many people have come. Today, we must ask ourselves how we honor our debt to them." *(Homily, September 7, 2008)*

Pedophilia: "If a priest is a pedophile, he carried that perversion in him before he was ordained. Changing the rule of celibacy would not treat such a perversion. Either you have it, or you don't. We need to be extremely prudent in our choice of candidates to the priesthood. The Seminary of Buenos Aires admits approximately 40 percent of applicants, and we follow the process attentively." *(Le jésuite, 2010)*

Progressivism: "If the Church wants to be progressive, . . . it has to acknowledge, and not deny, its historical heritage, and then move forward. If we say that in order to be progressive, the Church has to keep up with every passing ideology, then it will lose its identity and turn into an NGO." *(Press conference in Quebec, June 18, 2008)*

Single Mothers: "I say this with sadness, and if it sounds like a complaint or an offensive comment please forgive me: in our ecclesiastical region there are presbyteries that will not baptize children whose mothers are not married because the infants were conceived outside holy wedlock. They are the hypocrites of today. They clericalize the Church. They drive God's people away from salvation. And that poor girl who beat the temptation instilled by some in her to abort, who had the courage to bring her child into the world, then found herself on a pilgrimage, going from parish to parish, trying to find someone who would baptize her child." *(Homily, September 2012)*

Soccer: "I haven't missed a single San Lorenzo league game since 1946. The team's colors, blue and red, represent the Virgin's red dress and blue robe. We took the colors of the Virgin and no others." *(Le jésuite, 2010)*

Slavery: "This country accommodates the sale of slaves: men and women who buy and sell other people, violating their dignity. Let us ask God to touch the hearts of men and women who enslave, because they too are slaves. Slaves of cupidity, of pride, of vanity, and of evil." *(Homily, December 2008)*

Tango: "I really love to watch the tango danced by young people." *(Le jésuite, 2010)*

Truth: "We have been sent to preach the truth, to do good for all, and to bring joy to our people. It is not enough for our truth to be orthodox and our pastoral action efficient. Without the joy of beauty, truth becomes ruthless, cold, and prideful, which we see in the speech of the many bitter fundamentalists." *(Homily for the Chrismal Mass, April 21, 2011)*

(The preceding section, "Francis from A to T," appeared in the March 14, 2013, edition of the French newspaper *La Croix*.)

CHAPTER IV

The Pope We Have Been Waiting For

When Pope Francis's election was announced, all sorts of reactions arrived from around the globe, expressing enormous surprise and often great joy. The simplicity of the new pontiff's first words — as well as his first gestures — instantly raised tremendous hope. Without aiming to be exhaustive, the selection of testimonials gathered and presented below gives an idea of both the diversity of the Church and of its expectations, while at the same time greeting a personality many are looking forward to getting to know better.

He Was a Guide to the Poorest

It is impossible not to share in the joy and pride Argentinean Catholics felt when the great news was announced. Below, four of them express themselves with the simplicity of those who speak from the heart. The words that come most immediately to their tongues are "hope," "humility," and "presence."

"I was really moved when I learned that the new Father of the Church was our former cardinal, Jorge Bergoglio," says **Maria Constanza Fazio**, a lawyer. "I felt tremendous joy and was filled with hope, because it's the first time we have had a Latin American pope . . . let alone an Argentinean one! But it's not just the fact that he's an Argentine and has spent his life in this country that he referred to as 'the ends of the earth.' It's because he was a tremendous priest to his people, who unfortunately, still live in a situation of tremendous insecurity. He was a guide to the poorest, accompanying them in their daily lives with concrete, down-to-earth actions. He was always present in the most neglected towns and neighborhoods. In a gesture that was both grandiose and humble, he even washed the feet of the most downtrodden among them. The people who live in those neighborhoods, who have known him since childhood, or since his first steps as a pastor, are unanimous when it comes to judging him: he is a simple, humble man, whose vocation is deep and sincere.

"Latin Americans represent 40 percent of the world's Catholics, so it's only natural that the pope should come from here! In Argentina, Cardinal Bergoglio's pastoral activities were particularly attentive to the problems of the poor and to getting young people involved with the Church. That is worth its weight in gold. He has also repeatedly demonstrated his desire to unite people, whatever their religion may be.

"Even now, he is staying true to his values. Since he was

elected, he has continued to show his simplicity, and is bring-
ing a message of renewal: the Church has to change.

"As a Catholic, it gives me hope to know that that is the
path that God's right-hand man here on Earth is leading
the Church on to. The path of union for all men, especially
the poorest."

Adriana Martinez, a housewife, bears witness to the
cardinal's presence at difficult times. "We needed a priest to
give the sacrament of Holy Communion to a young woman
of thirty who had just had a terrible accident (it was after
that that she decided to convert to Catholicism and to be
baptized). Her condition was critical. She wound up pulling
through, but the consequences are terrible and irreversible:
she has been left entirely paralyzed; she can move only her
head and part of one arm.

"The priests we appealed to couldn't go to her because
she lived several miles away from Buenos Aires, the capital of
Argentina. One Sunday morning, I was reading *La Naciün,* a
newspaper here, and I came across an interview with Cardinal Jorge Mario Bergoglio, who was talking about his activities. And his e-mail address was given at the end of the ar-
ticle. Considering how urgent the situation was, we decided
to write to him to explain the young woman's case, but we
didn't know if anything would come of it. Ten days later, we
got a letter from the cardinal himself, asking us to check the
phone numbers in our e-mail, because he had been trying,
unsuccessfully, to reach us for several days. We answered,
and the very next day the cardinal called us. He wanted to

know more about the situation in order to help us. He gave us the names of several priests we could call, and he asked us to let him know personally if none of them could give Lucía communion. Well, we finally got what we wanted, and we are eternally grateful to him for his simplicity, his determination to help, and his presence at that difficult time.

"So I was very happy when I heard about his election, because I think that he will do an admirable job of representing God on Earth."

A member of the youth group in San Martín de Porres parish in Belgrano, Buenos Aires, **Gonzalo Castillo** is an engineer. What impressed him most about Cardinal Bergoglio was his vigorous sermons.

"Every year on Palm Sunday, Mass is celebrated in Flores Cathedral, or, to be precise, under the porch facing the street. And for the Feast of Corpus Christi, the same celebration is organized, but this time at the Cathedral of Buenos Aires. Both Masses are celebrated by the archbishop of Buenos Aires, that is, Cardinal Bergoglio, until now. For the past few years, Father José Luis Rey, the priest of San Martín de Porres — who is also a friend of mine — has been in charge of organizing that Mass. And every year, he asks me to give him a hand with that task.

"The cardinal presides over the Mass, and Father José Luis and I are seated next to him to accompany him during the celebration. What I've noticed at each of his sermons is a great firmness in denouncing injustice and negligence, particularly within our Church. He invites both Catholics and non-Catholics to step outside of their homes and to help people in need. In fact, his words are more than just invitations, they are firm and strong exhortations.

"I thank God for giving me the chance to get to know Cardinal Bergoglio — whom I really should start calling Pope Francis now — more personally during those two celebrations at San Martín de Porres. The first time was at the parish's saint's day celebration. It was a Saturday morning, and he was going to celebrate the eleven o'clock Mass, I think it was, but he got there about an hour early so he could talk to the young people of the parish first. He sat down facing us, and he spoke to us first. He answered our questions in all simplicity. Back then, our group of young parishioners was growing fast, and I remember that someone asked him, 'How are we going to keep all these young people busy?' And he answered, 'Let them be activists. Let them go into the streets and offer their services to anyone they find who is in need.' And he added, 'I meet a lot of young people who sit at home and wonder what their role in life is. Let them go out into the streets.'

"The second time I got to speak to him personally was last year, for the fiftieth anniversary of the canonization of San Martín de Porres. He had come to celebrate Mass in our parish again. I was standing at the door to the church that faces the street, doing the finishing touches, when I saw him walking quietly up. I greeted him, and then I escorted him to the parish's refectory. He sat down and had a *maté* with Father José Luis and some friends of mine, while I went back to finish what I had been doing. Both times that he came to the parish, we offered to have someone pick him up and drive him here, but he turned us down, swearing that he would rather take the subway and use the time to pray. Ever since he was elected pope, they've been talking about how he almost never goes anywhere by car, and I suppose that they've been repeating it so much that it's getting boring. But it's true: every time Pope Francis came to our parish, he took the subway.

"The last time I heard him speak, he was still cardinal, and he was talking to the catechists: 'When you receive a child who wants to start taking catechism, don't ask him if he's been baptized, or if his parents are married or divorced. Instead, ask him what he needs.'

"I really think that Pope Francis will be able to bring the Church closer to the faithful. He can bring the same honesty and simplicity that Jesus had. I don't think he'll be able to solve all the Church's problems; there are too many of them and they are too serious. But I am convinced that he incarnates the Church's renewal, a Church where the pope and the bishops are like a reflection of Jesus: simple men, missionaries, who know how to be both firm and merciful, who are close to the faithful, who eschew ostentation and whose motivations are irreproachable."

A student, **Clara Decurgez** belongs to the San Martín de Porres parish youth group, too. She had a chance to meet Monsignor Bergoglio as well. "What does Pope Francis represent for me? I would say that it's a surprise, and a source of pride and of hope. A surprise because I was absolutely not expecting him to be elected pope. I was stunned at first, and then it really moved me. A source of pride, because in my opinion, he represents the universal Church, not just Argentines, but Catholics from around the world who want to live and transmit their faith. And a source of hope for the Church, because I have great faith in both his judgment and his perseverance. He'll be able to sort out and confront the internal conflicts that, as a young practicing Catholic, were starting to upset me. And a source of hope for the rest of the world, too, because his sincere and truly Christian lifestyle will resonate around the world.

"I'm twenty-two years old, and I am lucky enough to have already met Pope Francis when he was still a bishop. He was always very discreet, and that's why the memories I have of the Masses he presided over at our church are kind of vague. If I had known he was going to be pope someday, I would have paid more attention! He's a humble man who knows how to project both firmness and clarity in his messages. He's very interested in young people, which is how he's kept a youthful spirit. He always encouraged and supported the missionary activities undertaken by young people in my parish. He's a man of action, who is devoted to the faithful, body and soul.

"It was really moving to see him on TV and in the newspapers, all dressed in white, under the headline 'Supreme Pontiff.' He seems very far away from me, yet at the same time very near — as though I'd seen my neighbor on TV. I guess I've always thought of him like a normal person, just like any one of the many worshipers in my parish.

"It's really heartwarming to see that with simple acts in daily life, and a coherent and faithful attitude toward Christ, you can go really far.

"I think I'm really lucky to have been able to attend Masses celebrated by the future Pope Francis, and to have been able to talk to him like an ordinary person, not like an audience or anything like that."

Communicative Enthusiasm!

During a trip to Argentina, **Father Stan Rougier** also had a chance to meet Monsignor Bergoglio. He remembers the cardinal's enthusiasm about programs for the poor that had been started in the slums surrounding Buenos Aires.

"It was in 1999, and at the time I was researching a book I was writing about Father Paco Huidobro (*Paco Huidobro, le prophète de Buenos Aires* [Salvator Publications, 2002]), who had been a friend of mine at the French Mission seminary. He was from Spain. A former miner, he was born into a Communist family, and at one time had been a member of the Communist Party himself. But he wound up deciding to become a worker-priest in Argentina. In the slums around the capital, he started all sorts of programs for the poor, distributing food and helping women whose husbands had abandoned them. Years before Coluche (a French actor and stand-up comedian who, in 1985, founded a nationwide chain of soup kitchens for the homeless, called Restaurants from the Heart), he founded veritable Restaurants from the Heart, and distributed food baskets to anyone who needed them. He displayed an uncommon devotion to Christ. He would bring the Holy Sacrament from house to house practically every Sunday.

"When I interviewed the archbishop, Monsignor Bergoglio, he struck me as someone who was extraordinarily enthusiastic about initiatives of solidarity like Paco's. He was an open, accessible man willing to listen for a long time, and eager to be informed about things he didn't know. The archbishop explained to me quite candidly that they couldn't even give Father Paco a curate to assist him, because no one else was willing to live so austerely. 'Your friend is a saint,' he confided in me discreetly. Paco has since gone to join his beloved Lord.

"You can judge people by whom they love, and I was struck by the goodness, sensitivity, and generosity toward others that the archbishop displayed. Some people categorize Monsignor Bergoglio on the conservative side, but I can testify to his admiration — and it was mutual — for that left-wing priest, who was devoted to serving people in the slums. Bear in mind that over the course of his episcopate, he doubled the number of priests serving the poorer, neglected neighborhoods. That's really something.

"A few years later, after his nomination to the cardinalship, the future pope gave a very brave homily for the anniversary of the May Revolution. 'The silent voices of so many dead cry out to us from heaven, beseeching us not to repeat the errors of the past. That is the only thing that can give meaning to their tragic fates.' So I absolutely do not understand why people are accusing him of having turned two priests in during the dictatorship, or criticizing him for having kept a 'culpable silence.' That seems absolutely unthinkable, unimaginable even, to me! We need to analyze the facts, the circumstances, and the context to be able to understand everyone's point of view, without leaping to conclusions.

"He chose the name Francis, as has been remarked upon quite a bit. Obviously, when you think of the saint from Assisi, you think of the fact that he chose austerity and took Dame Poverty as his bride. But don't forget that he also knew how to create an atmosphere of peace and serenity around him. The groups and communities that he founded or inspired have benefited from the messages of gentle caring that profoundly define who he is. And it is precisely that nonviolent spirit of peace and love that allowed for the profound transformation of the Church. Without resorting to overturning the hierarchy, Francis truly fostered a reconversion, a return to the Church's roots. The best way I can think of to describe the judiciousness of that approach is to quote Confucius: 'It's better to light a candle than to curse the darkness.'

"I have a heartfelt belief that the new pope will act in that spirit. Very gently, perhaps imperceptibly, he's going to make changes that we probably won't be around to see, but which will bear fruit much farther down the road."

For Someone Like Me . . .
More of a Christian Than a Catholic

A French novelist, and member of the Association of Religious Writers, **Cécilia Dutter** is particularly in touch with spiritual issues, and has written a book about Etty Hillesum. Right from the start, Francis's attitude moved her, and she sees it as a sign for the world in these times of crisis.

"The Argentinean cardinal Jorge Mario Bergoglio has just been elected by the conclave, taking the name of Francis I [*sic*], after Benedict XVI's unprecedented resignation on February 11. For someone like me, who sees herself more as a Christian than a Catholic, as I don't feel like I belong, strictly speaking, to a community but rather to a school of thought, a way of considering the world according to Christ and the gospel, I wasn't expecting the surge of emotion I felt when I saw the white smoke rise up from the Sistine Chapel. That evening, and despite all my prejudices, my eyes were glued to the TV along with those of every other Catholic on the planet. 'Habemus papam!' Yes, but *who?* Over an hour later, he appeared on the balcony of Saint Peter's Basilica, projecting, from the moment he stepped on to the 'world stage,' clearly visible signs of change.

"Gone were the pomp and circumstance we have come to expect. The choice of an incredibly plain white cassock — without the slightest ornamentation, combined with the reference to Francis of Assisi, the image of absolute humility, and, even more importantly, the reputation of this man, who is known for his fierce struggle against poverty, all lead me to believe that a new day is dawning with this pope from South America. In this period of economic crisis, how can we not see him as a glimmer of hope? Hope for a more equitable system of sharing the world's resources. As I see it, the Church's proper role is to stand up against today's laissez-faire economics. Pope Francis needs to lead by example, by staying close to the most vulnerable, and by providing assistance to them through his many pastoral and charitable networks. But more than anything else, in these times of spiritual crisis, in response to the failure of our society of overconsumption, which cannot make us happy since it is unable to fill our souls, it is impossible not to see this election as showing us that another path is possible. The path of returning to a kind of austerity, of greater value being placed on our interiority than on our appearance. So that is what I hope to see from this pope: over and above the noble and salutary struggle against poverty, I would like him to introduce the joy of the Essential to all those who have access to 'the material comforts,' and to lead mankind to an existential refocusing, an opening to the Infinite at the very heart of contingency. For that, I hope that he will leave dogmatism by the wayside and come back to the crystal-clear transparency of the Christian message. I would like this man, who the cardinal electors 'went to the ends of the earth' to find, to lead us toward that other side of the earth that is the spiritual dimension, by coming back to the simplicity and the purity of the original Word, which alone is able to truly speak to people's hearts. Perhaps then will I more easily feel like I belong to the great Catholic community that I am in communion with today."

What Can We Expect from a Jesuit Pope?

The unprecedented designation of a Supreme Pontiff who is a member of the Society of Jesus is an event in and of itself. So what will be the distinguishing characteristics, the specificity, of a man forged in the spirituality of Saint Ignatius of Loyola? What's more, what will they be of a pope who has chosen to be called Francis, as Father Etienne Grieu, who is also a Jesuit, points out? Superior general of the Society of Jesus, the **Very Reverend Adolfo Nicolás** greeted the appointment of Monsignor Bergoglio with great warmth:

> In the name of the Society of Jesus, I give thanks to God for the election of our new pope, Cardinal Jorge Mario Bergoglio, S.J., which opens for the Church a path full of hope.
>
> All of us Jesuits accompany with our prayers our brother and we thank him for his generosity in accepting the responsibility of guiding the Church at this crucial time. The name of "Francis" by which we shall now know him evokes for us the Holy Father's evangelical spirit of closeness to the poor, his identification with simple people, and his commitment to the renewal of the Church. From the very first moment in which he appeared before the people of God, he

gave visible witness to his simplicity, his humility, his pastoral experience, and his spiritual depth.

"The distinguishing mark of our Society is that it is . . . a companionship . . . bound to the Roman Pontiff by a special bond of love and service" (*Complementary Norms,* No. 2, §2). Thus, we share the joy of the whole Church, and at the same time, wish to express our renewed availability to be sent into the vineyard of the Lord, according to the spirit of our special vow of obedience, that so distinctively unites us with the Holy Father (*General Congregation* 35, Decree 1, No. 17).

P. Adolfo Nicolás, S.J.
Superior General

"The fact that Jorge Mario Bergoglio has chosen 'Francis' as his name truly delights me," exclaims **Father Etienne Grieu**, "because it expresses his desire for a return to the gospel in all its strength and simplicity, a return that the Church needs to make again and again, constantly. One can also see it as the incarnation of the clear affinity that exists between Ignatian spirituality and the Franciscan tradition: an attachment to Christ as a person, and to the poor and humiliated Christ, are, I think, essential components of the process in the Spiritual Exercises of Ignatius of Loyola. That was also the face of Jesus that was strongly highlighted by the *Poverello* of Assisi. They naturally go hand in hand with paying particular attention to those who are ignored or kept out of bounds by our performance- and efficiency-obsessed societies.

"What specific touches can we expect from a Jesuit pope? It's a bit risky to hazard any overly precise guesses, since Jorge Mario Bergoglio will obviously have his own personal way of understanding and living the Ignatian tradition. As far as I'm concerned, there's one key thing, but we'll have to wait and see if it's relevant in Francis's case: the Ignatian perspective leads to 'seeing God in all things.' At least, that's what we see in the 'Contemplation to Attain Love,' which constitutes one of the summits of the set of Spiritual Exercises (exercises 230 to 237). At that point in the journey, a relationship with God starts to become established that is both eminently personal ('I am grateful for all the gifts received, for the call to existence that I benefit from') and, at the same time, much broader, because it is part of the immense movement of creation and redemption that labors in the world. The believer is urged to inscribe his reply to God — which is to offer and give everything that he has and is into God's hands — within the dynamic that is entirely beyond him. In this way, the ever-tempting dichotomy between interior life and presence in the world, which causes Christian faith to lose so much of its strength, is circumvented.

"On the contrary, that exercise calls forth an intensified sensitivity to the events of the world, particularly when people or groups are suffering or abandoned, as well as a way of being interested in them: not only a distanced analysis — which is still indispensable nevertheless — but also a combat in which God's presence and his passion for his creation is at stake. That could color the Church's social discourse with a more spiritual touch, echoing and accentuating the line initiated by Benedict XVI with *Deus caritas est* and *Caritas in veritate.*"

In the Footsteps of a Free Man

He chose to call himself Francis, as a direct reference to Saint Francis of Assisi, one of the most popular saints in history, and one who still speaks to our contemporaries through his concern for the poor, for peace, for dialogue, and for respect for nature. **Father Michel Hubaut**, a Franciscan, has high hopes that this evangelical inspiration will have a great influence on the Church of the future.

" 'Go, Francis, and repair my house, which as you see is falling into ruin.' The instant the pope's choice of name was announced, I immediately thought of the crucified Christ in the Chapel of San Damiano calling out to Francis of Assisi. In and of itself, the name asserts a strong evangelical message: an affirmation of the values of love and sharing. Even if the pope, from where he stands, will not have as much latitude, as much freedom, as the *Poverello* of Assisi did, the choice still clearly points things in a certain direction. Toward simplicity, of course, in order to lighten up the weight of splendor, or even to renounce all pomp. The better to inhabit the simplicity of the gospel. Cardinal Bergoglio's journey illustrates this attention to the poor and the downtrodden very well. That ideal should lead to greater transparency, notably in the Vatican's finances, a subject that the media have been having a field day with of late.

"As we know, Francis of Assisi showed tremendous respect to other people; he put great trust in them. I hope that the new pope will put the same trust in the episcopal conferences on different continents, and that the Church will be governed in a less centralized way, so that reflections and initiatives can circulate widely.

"For his time, Francis was quite innovative, in that he met the Sultan for a discussion about Islam: for him, every man is the Word of God, in the broadest sense of the term. That attitude should guide our new pope to openness to new cultures. In my opinion, he needs to manage to stimulate and encourage rather than to condemn; to be a source of support rather than a stern judge. Why not adopt less severe jurisprudence toward remarried divorcées, for instance? The pope has already used the terms 'journey' and 'path' several times; he needs to know how to propose a direction, a path, a teaching that will create stepping stones toward God. For the Church must not remain focused in on itself; it is neither God nor Christ, nor the kingdom; it must show us the way toward them. Let's listen to Francis of Assisi, who spoke of 'walking in the footsteps of our Lord Jesus Christ.'

"The concept of belief-based teaching would be in the spirit of Francis, a free man, and I wish our new pope the same freedom. In a more open, less uptight Church, he needs to find the courage to create new ministries, to be bold enough to step out of the medieval ecclesiastical framework in order to reconnect with people of today. I get the feeling that his first gestures are a step in that direction."

A Latino Pope: It's Novel and Normal!

A pope who hails from the New World, a Latino pope, what could that change or bring about? The Dominican **Alain Durand**, president of the Friends of DIAL (Distribution of Information about Latin America), is very familiar with the South American continent and with issues related to poverty.

"A 'Latino pope' is both absolutely novel and absolutely normal. Absolutely novel, because it's the first time — not in two thousand years, which is meaningless, but since the Spanish Conquest in the sixteenth century — and yet, nothing could be more normal, since Latin America is the continent where 40 percent of the world's Catholics now live.

"Our Latino brothers are obviously thrilled about this election, but what it will mean for them may actually be somewhat ambiguous. I can't tell you how many times I've heard Latin American friends gloat about the one great advantage they had over Christians in Old World Europe: being far away from Rome. A relative advantage, surely, but a real one nevertheless. Relative because we all know that, after twenty-seven years' worth of John Paul II's episcopal nominations in Latin America, the conservative — or at best moderate — majority now has a clear hold on the hierarchy. Not long ago, I heard one of the last 'great bishops' of the continent say, perfectly humbly, that for some time now, Rome had been appointing mediocre people only, in order to avoid trouble.

"Now, with Pope Francis, Rome will be closer to Latin America. Only the future will tell if the continent will gain from having closer ties to the Holy See.

"Personally, I'm not expecting anything new from the new archbishop of Rome in terms of doctrine or morals. As far as I am aware, this pope defends a traditional standpoint on all the controversial questions. My one hope is that neither he, nor the press, will get fixated on issues about different forms of sexuality, same-sex marriage, contraception, respecting just-fertilized eggs, etc.

"For me, there's something much more urgent and serious to worry about in today's world: the scope of the poverty in which hundreds of millions of our contemporaries live. And on that score, I think we can expect quite a bit from this pope, because he has already taken brave stands on the subject and has put his money where his mouth is, as it were. What I find absolutely remarkable about the man is that he doesn't separate his personal living conditions from his convictions in terms of social justice. He knows how to live modestly, humbly, and close to those who are subjected to inhumane living conditions. I sincerely hope that neither the pomp and splendors of the Vatican, nor the pressure of the Curia, will put paid to his determination.

"As he has often declared loudly and clearly, he believes

that poverty, in and of itself, is a human-rights violation. The idea is not to honor poor people by adopting or advocating an admiring, practically contemplative attitude toward them — as seems to be becoming more and more fashionable in our country — but to fight against poverty alongside the poor. A pope who comes from the heart of the most dramatic problem in today's world, one that is a source of so much suffering and humiliation, deserves our respect and support.

"The media pointed out Pope Francis's extremely worrying behavior when he was Superior of the Jesuits during the Argentinean dictatorship. For me, that was a serious question mark. On the one hand, we know that the Argentinean episcopate was one of the worst ones in Latin America, in terms of their relationship to the dictatorial regime (1976-83). And of course, he has since publicly expressed regret for his behavior. But what exactly was going on with the Provincial Superior of the Jesuits, a religious order that has shown great courage in its solidarity with the poor?

"Some people have accused the current pope of having abandoned two Jesuit priests living in an underprivileged neighborhood to their plight in the hands of the junta. Several people, including one eminent specialist, stood by that story, without any convincing proof, it seemed to me, which is surprising, considering who it was coming from. So I was looking forward to hearing what Adolfo Perez Esquivel, the Argentinean Nobel Peace Prize winner, had to say. I was sure he would react to the accusations quite soon, since he is perhaps the most ardent defender of human rights in Latin

America. He was personally subjected to torture under the Argentinean dictatorship, and it was a miracle that he escaped the tragic fate of those who were thrown into the sea from the notorious 'death flights.'

"Perez Esquivel's position is extremely clear, which is truly reassuring to me. He stated quite emphatically in an interview with the BBC (on March 14): 'Some bishops were accomplices to the dictatorship, but not Bergoglio. People are accusing Bergoglio, saying he didn't do what needed to be done to get two Jesuits out of jail while he was Superior of the Jesuit congregation. But I know perfectly well that a lot of bishops asked the military junta to free prisoners and priests and that the requests were not granted. Nothing ties him to the dictatorship.' Adolfo Perez Esquivel is not the kind of person to kowtow when it comes to human rights. This whole business can't help but remind me of the accusations of Nazism made against the so-called 'panzer cardinal' Ratzinger when he was elected pope. The press, sometimes even the legitimate press, can't resist gossip!

"Will Pope Francis manage to escape the pitfalls of the Vatican? For now, we can certainly hope so! As Dom Pedro Casaldaliga — another Latin American bishop, who recently received death threats for defending indigenous peoples from those who would steal their lands — has said, we need to do away with Vatican City State, a symbol of power and wealth that has no connection whatsoever to the gospel. It's one thing for the Queen of England to maintain an opulent purple-and-gold façade, but quite another for the Catholic

Church to do the same thing. That's the real problem. What should be done? Why not start three-way negotiations between the Vatican, Italy, and UNESCO, the objective of which would be to place that fabulous cultural heritage for humanity under international jurisdiction? It would be the perfect occasion to trim back the Curia's mammoth bureaucracy. A pope who chose to live in an ordinary apartment and have an office in a working-class neighborhood . . . what a great leap forward that would represent toward the emergence of that 'poor and servant' Church that good old Pope John used to talk about.

"I'd like to end with an in-joke: here's a Jesuit pope who has donned the white robes that the popes inherited from the Dominicans. What a wonderful symbol of fraternity between those who labor for the gospel!

"The future still holds great promise."

Lofty Goals for the Church

Theologians are of course observing the advent of Pope Francis with great interest, and are carefully scrutinizing the first words, gestures, and symbols he chooses, in order to extract their full meaning. That is the case with **Father Laurent Villemin**, a professor at the *Theologicum,* the Faculty of Theology and Religious Sciences at the Catholic Institute of Paris.

"The appearance of a new pope on Saint Peter's benediction loggia is always a moment of both expectation and joy — the joy of having a new pope and the apprehension of having to wait and see who he really is and what he will do. Behind their apparent simplicity, those few words pronounced by Pope Francis just after his election on the evening of March 13 already offer a glimpse of a whole theology of the Church.

"Not once did he pronounce the word 'pope' or 'Supreme Pontiff.' He introduced himself as the bishop of Rome, and he referred to that office several times: 'You know that it was the duty of the conclave to give Rome a bishop.' 'The diocesan community of Rome now has its Bishop. Thank you! And first of all, I would like to offer a prayer for our Bishop Emeritus, Benedict XVI.' He refers to his predecessor as 'Bishop Emeritus' and not 'Pope Emeritus' — even though that is the title that was bestowed upon him after his resignation. The symbolism is eloquent, too: although he did wear the white cassock, he didn't wear the scarlet *mozzetta* — that little ermine-lined cape that is the symbol of pontifical power. He also kept his bishop's pectoral cross, rather than donning the solid-gold cross that had been readied for him. Of course, it's a sign of humility, but it is also rich in ecclesiological signification.

"And then the pope went on, 'And now, we take up this journey: Bishop and People. This journey of the Church of Rome.... A journey of fraternity, of love, of trust among us. Let us always pray for one another.' Doing so, he revealed his conception of the episcopacy, which is based on a fundamental bond with the people who are confided to him to travel a path together. What's more, doing exactly as he said, before he gave the throngs his blessing, he bowed his head and said, 'I ask a favor of you: before the Bishop blesses his people, I ask you to pray to the Lord that he will bless me: the prayer of the people asking the blessing for their Bishop. Let us make this prayer in silence: your prayer over me.' A bishop who requests a prayer from his flock before blessing them in turn? How can we not be reminded of Saint Augustine preaching to his flock on the anniversary of his consecration: 'Let me therefore have the assistance of your prayers, that the one who did not disdain to bear with me may also deign to bear my burden with me. . . . For you, I am a bishop; with you, after all, I am a Christian' (Sermon 340).

"In so doing, Bishop Francis not only draws a theology for the bond between the bishop of Rome and his people of the diocese of Rome, he reveals his way of seeing the diocesan Church and its ties with its bishop, and shows the importance that he grants to diocesan churches, local churches.

"In the run-up to the conclave, several cardinals expressed their desire for local churches to have a larger role. Pope Francis's first words showed that he took that request to heart — a request that is, after all, founded on great Church tradition, and which was reiterated strongly by the Second Vatican Council, most notably in its *Lumen gentium* Dogmatic Constitution on the Church. Section 23 of that constitution refers to the intrinsic bond between the universal Church and the local churches (dioceses). [This is why each individual bishop represents his own church, but all of them together and with the pope represent the entire Church in the bond of peace, love, and unity — Trans.] But putting this principle into practice has always been more problematic. . . . Since Gregory VII in the ninth century, the Church has been marked by a tremendous centralization of power. The Second Vatican Council sowed hope that local churches would regain legitimate autonomy, but, fifty years later, we can't really say that there has been a true inculturation of the government, the Word of God, or the liturgy. . . . So above and beyond his inaugural speech, this will be a challenge for the pontificate of this new pope.

"Because many current issues simply cannot be resolved on a planetary level, it would be perfectly possible for a decision to be taken in one place and not in another. A lot of churches, for instance, have already worked on welcoming remarried divorcées at the Eucharist. The idea would be to see how their experience could be shared and applied in some places. The point is not to weaken the figure of the pope, but to work out how his unifying ministry can continue to play a strong part while at the same time giving real responsibility to individual churches.

"By choosing to identify himself first as a 'bishop,' Pope Francis is also expressing his intention to honor the episcopacy once again. The risk in that case, however, is to see the pope as a single person, whereas Vatican II and history show a pope whose responsibility is deeply rooted in the College of Bishops. According to the definition in *Lumen gentium* (section 22), there is an intrinsic and dynamic bond between the episcopal college and the pope's unique office. 'Just as in the Gospel, the Lord so disposing, St. Peter and the other apostles constitute one apostolic college, so in a similar way the Roman Pontiff, the successor of Peter, and the bishops, the successors of the apostles, are joined together.' This conception of the primacy of the Roman pontiff in the midst of the College of Bishops is a strong message toward the Orthodox Churches, as was the expression used by Francis, *'The Church of Rome, which presides in charity over all the Churches.'* This is not just a change of title, but a whole ecclesiology that is being developed here and in the rest of his speech.

"This, the pope's first address from the loggia, is not addressed only to Romans and the diocesan Church of Rome, and the pope knows that perfectly well. The whole of the Church has not been forgotten. The pope is the bishop of Rome first, and it is on the strength of the role of that Church, founded in the blood of the martyrs Peter and Paul, that the bishop of Rome plays a singular role in the universal Church. This is an extremely traditional theology, because the expression 'preside in charity' was first used to describe the Church of Rome by Saint Ignatius of Antioch in the early second century. And those were in fact the very words used by Benedict XVI during the Angelus on February 19, 2012, for the Feast of the Chair of Saint Peter: 'At the beginning of the second century Saint Ignatius of Antioch attributed a special primacy to the Church which is in Rome, greeting her in his *Letter to the Romans* as the one which "presides in charity." It is because the Apostles Peter and Paul, together with many other martyrs, poured out their blood in this City, that this special task of service depends on the Community of Rome and on its Bishop. Let us, thus, return to the witness of blood and of charity. The Chair of Peter is therefore the sign of authority, but of Christ's authority, based on faith and on love.' Highlighting that on the very first time he spoke as pope shows a clear will to institute a different kind of relationship with the local churches, and, implicitly, with the other Christian churches.

"One is indeed struck by the proximity of these words to those of John Paul II's encyclical letter *Ut unum sint* (1995), about the unity of Christians. That encyclical included a whole passage about the office of the bishop of Rome, most notably about his bond with the other bishops: 'When the Catholic Church affirms that the office of the Bishop of Rome corresponds to the will of Christ, she does not separate this office from the mission entrusted to the whole body of Bishops, who are also "vicars and ambassadors of Christ." The Bishop of Rome is a member of the "College," and the Bishops are his brothers in the ministry' (*Ut unum sint* §95). There is no doubt that Pope Francis is ready to adopt the words of his predecessor in that same encyclical letter: 'When addressing the Ecumenical Patriarch His Holiness Dimitrios I, I acknowledged my awareness that "for a great variety of reasons, and against the will of all concerned, what should have been a service sometimes manifested itself in a very different light. But . . . it is out of a desire to obey the will of Christ truly that I recognize that as Bishop of Rome I am called to exercise that ministry. . . . I insistently pray the Holy Spirit to shine his light upon us, enlightening all the Pastors and theologians of our Churches, that we may seek — together, of course — the forms in which this ministry may accomplish a service of love recognized by all concerned"' (§95).

"The introduction to the Blessing that closes the first speech on the loggia shows that Pope Francis's church doesn't conceive of itself for itself but for 'all men and women of good will,' for all of humanity. 'Now I will give the Blessing to you and to the whole world, to all men and women of good will.' The expression 'all men and women of good will' is a discreet reference to the introduction to John XXIII's encyclical letter *Pacem in terris.* Lofty goals indeed!"

A Pastoral Marked with Simplicity

Cardinal Barbarin, archbishop of Lyon, participated in the last two conclaves, where he had a chance to get to know Monsignor Bergoglio when he was still archbishop of Buenos Aires. The French cardinal is outspoken in his admiration for the tremendous simplicity of the Argentine's pastoral approach, which suits people of today.

"His attitude is clear! Right from the start, Pope Francis introduced himself as bishop of Rome, paying homage to his predecessor as Bishop Emeritus of the City, and visiting Santa Maria Maggiore, one of Rome's major basilicas, right away. But as a pastor, I get the feeling that he's still very attached to Argentina, especially to his diocese, Buenos Aires. Staying close to ordinary people still really matters to him.

"How would I define his pastoral options? They are based on a very down-to-earth but powerful approach. For example, in his diocese, he launched a major baptism campaign! For him, that's the real way into the Church, a way of welcoming the greatest number of people, and we should focus on that initiatory sacrament. So they really went all-out over there: slogans, posters, a whole campaign, kind of like we do for the donation drive! 'Don't be afraid: baptize your children!' It seems that the campaign was very warmly welcomed by young parents, and attracted attention among Christians generally. Monsignor Bergoglio is obviously overwhelmingly concerned with the idea of keeping religion popular, in the original sense of the word, that is, for the people, without any of the folklore nonsense or pejorative connotations that the word can have. Once again, that strikes me as being simple, sound, and wholesome.

"Another example of the simplicity of his action as a bishop can be found in his focus on prayer, those 'weapons of prayer and sacrifice' that the young Thérèse of Lisieux spoke of. During the struggle with the Argentinean government about same-sex marriage, the cardinal even asked contemplative communities to pray in support of that difficult combat, and wrote to them to ask for an act of confidence in God through supplication. It was a wonderful way to include the conventual world in his work as a bishop.

"The other thing that I find very moving is that despite his thinking big and having lofty goals for his bishopric, he managed to maintain a true, personal contact with ordinary people. I've seen it for myself, with people we both know, especially the Argentinean nuns who live in the diocese of Lyon. And when a friend of mine, a young man in Buenos Aires, was going through a difficult period of depression and loneliness, I knew I could count on Monsignor Bergoglio to lend a hand. My friend got in touch with him, and the archbishop gave him the name of a priest he could talk to. That down-to-earth side, that concern for others, that's all you need to know about him. It makes him easy to get to know.

"And that down-to-earth side often comes along with a real sense of humor. I remember how he came up to me the day I participated in an encounter for the Congregation of the Liturgy for the first time. It's a rather solemn institution, as you can imagine. I was presenting a theological paper to a group of renowned experts, so I was pretty nervous. The minute it was over, he came up to me. 'Well,' he said. 'I'd heard that the Archbishop of Lyon really had faith, and I'm glad to see it's true!' And after he broke the ice like that, we had a truly profound theological discussion, without any gossip or small talk, which doesn't always happen in situations like that. And then we saw that down-to-earth side again after the conclave, when Francis stayed with the cardinals for breakfast, in all simplicity — or as if he wasn't really ready to move into his new quarters yet. Like he just wanted to enjoy this moment of conviviality with his brother cardinals.

"Is it thanks to the fact that the atmosphere was so much less troubled? His election did have the advantage of coming at a less dramatic time than Benedict XVI's — which, after all, followed John Paul II's death after a long illness. When the meeting of the congregations got started, we were a little bit worried at first that the date of the conclave might be moved forward. We didn't want to rush things, and I believe that we were right. We got to take our time, let the brother cardinals get beyond the shock and disappointment and gradually turn our thoughts to the future. After a few days, the exchange of information had been sufficient to enlighten us, and we were able to set the date for a conclave opening the following Tuesday. But the time we took to really listen to each other, and to get to the bottom of some of the issues and problems that we have been dealing with lately, was extremely useful. It allowed everyone's ideas to ripen and crystallize, and I think that's what enabled a fairly quick election and a result that I believe satisfied the largest possible number.

"To get back to Pope Francis's pastoral approach, I think it makes a really clear statement that he wants to avoid a self-centered — or 'self-referential,' to use his own word — Church, but one that is founded on and renewed in Christ. It is meant first and foremost to be for the faithful, in whose hearts the love of God unfolds. We mustn't try to uphold it for its own sake.

"That same simplicity has guided Monsignor Bergoglio in his attitude in the political arena, which we know has led to some debate and even criticism. But he was not in fact hostile to the principle of liberation theology: the idea of a liberating God is a constant in the Bible, and in the Our Father we even ask to be delivered from evil. Nor is it absurd for him to talk about Christ the liberator. But he was trying to be absolutely sure that things didn't get out of hand or go too far. He didn't want the Church to become the front for a political or ideological movement, nor to give in to the temptation of violence, no matter what the regime. If we measure his concern for freedom and resistance carefully, the balance comes out in his favor. And I couldn't help noticing that the Argentinean people seemed much more joyful about Pope Francis's election than Mrs. Kirchner did.

"In one of his first homilies as pope, he asked us quite vigorously to hold on, to make our faith last, despite the shadows that can darken our lives. But even in the darkness, in the worst moments, you have to know how to persevere. I'm not talking about the power of positive thinking or whatnot, but rather about being able to find a way to await the Lord confidently. It can happen that on our journey through life, the shadows are dispersed. And on that journey, even if we are living stones, even if we confess faith, we can still trip and fall, like Peter during the passion. Then we must put everything below Christ's cross, in all truth and simplicity.

"How can we not be inspired by such a bracing message of faith?"

We Are Hoping for a Benevolent Pope

Former vice-rector of the Catholic University in Leuven, Belgium, a priest and a writer, **Father Gabriel Ringlet** sees himself primarily as a specialist in communication. He decrypts for us the first images that the new pope offered to the world. Perhaps they herald a new way for the Church to address contemporary cultures.

"Like many people, I was greatly surprised by Pope Francis's appointment. Of course, like all the observers, we prepared files, and drew up lists of *papabile* (likely candidates for the succession), but his name was way down in fifteenth place, even after a few others from South America, like Cardinal Scherer. Although I have to admit that we media people have short memories! Because we all knew with near certainty that the Argentinean prelate had gotten nearly forty votes in the conclave before this one. Which means he was clearly admired by his peers. But oddly enough, that more historical information didn't come out in the media this time around.

"Personally, I thought it was very moving that he chose the first name Francis. First of all, it's a lovely name in and of itself, and I would say, as the Bible says, that you 'walk toward your name,' in order to fulfill its promise and live within it. In that sense, the new pope has set the bar quite high by referring to Francis of Assisi! I'm even going to go out on a limb and say that, symbolically, in a way, it's as though the 'Very Lowly,' who is written about so beautifully by the

French writer Christian Bobin — who was able to meet the cardinal in Latin America in connection with his work for the poor — was suddenly in the Vatican, up there with the Very High and Mighty! That strikes me as a really amazing sign, in spiritual terms. So now we just have to wait and see if Pope Francis is really going to manage to bring the presence of the Very Lowly — his lifestyle, hitherto — into the more rarefied atmosphere of the Vatican.

"Francis of Assisi displayed a great openness to fragility, but also to diversity. Let's not forget his encounter with the sultan — one of the first interfaith dialogues on historical record. It was also the meeting of two kinds of fragility. Is Pope Francis aware of having donned the garb of that ecumenical dimension and that broader vision as well?

"Of course, I'm pleased that before getting caught up in the internal issues, the pope is focusing on social morality, on the struggle against inequality, which he has raised to the status of a human-rights issue. What I hope is that that won't lead to too wide a gap between two morals — between those of social doctrine that go back to the Church's grand tradition and the morals that affect individuals' private lives, their personal fragility and their immense pain and suffering, in a very concrete way. I hope with all my heart that this Francis will be inhabited by that dual dimension.

"To do that, he will have to make a few bold gestures, the most obvious being opening Communion to remarried divorcées. Why not make that gesture, which would have such a huge impact? Even as I'm saying that, I can't help thinking of a young divorcée I know who is preparing her seven-year-old son for his first Communion, and of his question: 'But, Mommy, why can't you come to Communion with me?' Their situation makes me terribly sad, and I would so like to see it change!

"As a man of communication, I was struck by the first images of Francis on the balcony. Of course, we all know that communication issues were often problematic during the last pontificate. In those first few seconds right after he appeared, he seemed very serious, and a bit tense. Who wouldn't be? But it didn't take him at all long to relax, and very soon he started speaking in a straightforward, fraternal way — as though he were speaking to a few dozen people and not tens of thousands! We felt close to him, and that's what the Italian press meant when they described him as a 'brother Pope.'

"We saw some huge changes, real breaks with tradition on that occasion: instead of the pope immediately blessing the people, he bowed his head, and knelt to ask them to bless him. What a switch! That reminded me of a more personal anecdote that touched me quite profoundly. When I met the first woman rabbi of Brussels in church one day, she offered to give me her blessing. The simplicity of the pope's gesture struck me as being both very powerful and very moving.

"In that sense, he is already fulfilling the hopes of people, because we really need a pope who is full of compassion and benevolence, even if his pontificate doesn't last very long.

"Nevertheless, we have seen that those first, encouraging

signs haven't kept the press from jumping all over him right away — they have been particularly critical of his so-called 'collaborationist' attitude during the years of the Argentinean dictatorship, and of his recent opposition to same-sex marriage. It is pretty amazing to see how, in some media, the honeymoon period hardly lasted for more than a few minutes, and how appointing a pope reactivates some harshly secular reactions. As far as I'm concerned, we should give him the benefit of the doubt, and not jump to hasty conclusions, especially not without proof. Let's give him a little time to show us what he's going to do.

"From a more general point of view, no one can say what to expect from this pope without knowing who his secretary of state will be, for instance, and all those who will be working alongside him, at least until we have heard what his intentions are. Without necessarily having come up with a 'ticket' or an agreement as to who will be appointed to govern, I think the prelates at least have an idea in their minds about the context, a broad picture of the situation to help them choose.

"And the last two key ideas are the Church's relationship to modern culture and Church governance. And those two issues are intertwined, in my opinion.

"First of all, it is essential to take today's culture and anthropology into account, and even to adapt to the reality of different cultures! There's actually a tremendous amount at stake in this issue of the need for inculturation! But don't forget, our man is a Jesuit, and one of the specificities of the sons of Saint Ignatius of Loyola lies precisely in their capacity for adapting Christianity. Think of those great Jesuit figures who looked toward the Orient, like François Xavier and Matteo Ricci, who opened up the roads to China and Japan, and learned about the language, the mores, and the people they discovered . . . without forgetting the technical and scientific dimensions.

"And finally, there's the issue of governance of the Church: on that score, we have just experienced a historic event, insofar as Benedict XVI's resignation loosened tongues. Whichever concerns emerge as the new priorities, change is coming. This freeing up of speech represents real progress, and from now on, it will be taken for granted. Benedict XVI's dramatic deed led to an intense, salutary debate, and the atmosphere seems to have been quite different from the one preceding his election. The now emeritus pope has created an opening that is tantamount to sounding an alarm about how the Church is run, while at the same time allowing the cardinals to discuss the future. You can't go back again. It should lead to a real reform of the Curia, in a spirit that illustrates a warmer style."

An "Unhoped For" Waiting Period

When the opening of the conclave was announced, **Marie-Laure Carrière**, a lawyer with a degree in theology, was in the south of France on business. On the spur of the moment, she decided to fly to Rome. It was a chance for her to live a moment of grace.

"A trial in Nice, snow in Paris . . . and all roads lead to Rome! How could you not have faith? Faith leads to bearing witness. 'What a free spirit!' a fellow lawyer exclaims at the airport when I decide to stop waiting indefinitely for a flight to Paris, and to fly to Rome instead. In hindsight, I can see that I was being guided by a pure gift of the Holy Spirit, without an ounce of free will on my part. The Eternal City opened its doors to me just as those of the Sistine Chapel were closing.

"In the nonstop rain, the wait was a unique ecclesial experience, from the first black smoke early in the first evening all the way to the appearance of the chosen one twenty-four hours later, just as the rain had miraculously stopped.

"It was a day of prayer and predictions alongside Sister Catherine Aubin, a Dominican sister and journalist for Radio Vatican, and other journalists in France Television's office or outside a press room. Rumor had it that the election would be for that very night, but that it would be an Italian pope, most likely Cardinal Scola, according to those who supposedly had inside information. As an old hand at rhetoric, I insisted that it wouldn't be until the next day, because it was raining too hard, and the Holy Spirit couldn't possibly give us a new pope in such a downpour. And that it couldn't be a European; it was bound to be someone from somewhere else. I was hoping for a bold gesture from the cardinals, and, with a utopian outlook, I was picturing the Filipino, Cardinal Tagle, who had taken out two pages in the last issue of the *Journal du Dimanche* newspaper. In addition to his qualities as a pastor, which the media have saluted unanimously, he graduated summa cum laude, and his doctoral thesis on episcopal collegiality according to Vatican II seemed to offer hope for a concrete application of the Council. But my theological-apprentice-level analysis didn't seem to convince anyone.

"After an interlude buzzing with joyful journalists' anecdotes — Cardinal Barbarin being filmed sending one last text message as the French cardinals were driven to the conclave — it was time to get back to basics: prayer. And because the others had wound up convincing me that the white smoke was imminent, I hoped to be well informed by staying inside Saint Peter's Basilica, whose doors would remain ineluctably closed until the usual time if the vote were positive. So through a bit of a ruse, I managed to get right up front, staring right at the Swiss Guard, near the authorities . . . and next to an Argentinean woman who made me cry.

"The rain stopped; the seagull freed the chimney it had occupied for so long and the thick white smoke unfurled over Saint Peter's Square. The Church was magnificent, surpassing its weaknesses. Reinforced by the first words of our Pope Francis, it was a model of possible communication in cultural diversity. All those eyes gazing toward the same horizon. . . . What joy to have experienced that moment! With a startled look on his face, as though he was surprised by the crowd, then opening with a fraternal *'buona sera'* . . . calling upon us to pray for the emeritus bishop and kneeling to the faithful: you could tell that this was no ordinary pope in no time. Paying extra attention in order to try to decipher his words in Italian, getting confirmation from the improvised interpreters around me, I immediately saw this man who introduced himself as the bishop of Rome as the key to opening the Church to the world.

"Attentive to the Church's mission in favor of the poor, firmly established at the heart of the episcopal college, he should incarnate unity; thus the Church — instead of turning in on itself — appears, in the diversity of its members and as a communion of local, visible, and spiritual churches, as the historical reality gathered together and unified by Christ, bearing witness to the actuality of redemption. Let there be the possibility of communion, unity in diversity and against uniformity, and an astonishing sense of hope for a world in despair. That is my most devout wish. And why not use new technologies to help achieve all that? The Vatican seems to have outdone itself in terms of communication ever since the resignation."